Praise for *The Assault on the State*

"Contemporary authoritarians attack the modern, bureaucratic state as a threat; the 'deep' state, they argue, strangles the liberty of citizens and is meant to thwart their 'real' representatives. In this book two eminent political scientists show how disingenuous and dangerous such claims are. Attacks on the state, Professors Kopstein and Hanson show, should be seen as a means to an end – a tool modern authoritarians use to colonize the state with their cronies and undermine its ability to check their abuses of power. *The Assault on the State* is a much-needed addition to our understanding of the ways would-be authoritarians undermine democracy and consolidate their power."

Sheri Berman, Barnard College, Columbia University

"While scholars and commentators debate the global crisis of democracy, Hanson and Kopstein warn us of an even worse emergency: the return of patrimonialism and the assault on the modern state. From the US to the UK, from Russia to Hungary, from Brazil to Turkey, an unholy alliance of extreme libertarians, religious nationalists, and supporters of strong executive power threatens to undo a host of fundamental achievements that are central to our existence and that are the product of a functioning state. This is an essential book for understanding the current global political conjuncture."

Giovanni Capoccia, Professor of Comparative Politics, University of Oxford

"In this extraordinarily important book, Stephen Hanson and Jeffrey Kopstein go beyond the contemporary concerns about the state of modern democracy to demonstrate how the increasing attacks on government bureaucracies threaten our health, safety, security, and prosperity. They argue that three decades after outlasting the Soviet Union, the West is falling prey to the spread of corrupt Vladimir Putin-wannabes seeking to emulate Russia's path to personalistic rule by taking advantage of popular grievances. Hanson and Kopstein close by providing guidance to help us avoid returning to the vagaries of the pre-modern world."

James Goldgeier, American University

"The state is under attack, with ominous consequences for our safety, our democracy, and our livelihoods. This is an incisive, thoughtful, and spirited analysis of how personalist rule is assaulting and replacing the state: and what we can do about it. A must-read."

Anna Grzymala-Busse, Stanford University

"A thoughtful and probing discussion of the great challenges facing the democratic state. Powerful and exceptionally well-researched, *The Assault on the State* has enormous implications for governance in the modern era."

Don Kettl, The University of Texas at Austin

"In this sobering book, Hanson and Kopstein cogently explain why defending the administrative state from would-be political 'father figures' is the key battle of our times. From Putin's Russia to Orban's Hungary to Trump's America and beyond, the rule of law finds itself under attack by the rule of men. Only through clear-eyed recognition of the challenge and concerted, immediate action can we preserve the vital public agencies and services that we all too often take for granted."

Juliet Johnson, McGill University

"A powerful and important account of attacks on the administrative state by elected officials in the West. A must-read for anyone troubled by the state of democracy in our world."

Elton Skendaj, Georgetown University

THE ASSAULT ON THE STATE

The Assault on the State

*How the Global Attack on Modern
Government Endangers Our Future*

STEPHEN E. HANSON

JEFFREY S. KOPSTEIN

polity

First published in 2024 by Polity Press

Polity Press
65 Bridge Street
Cambridge CB2 1UR, UK

Polity Press
111 River Street
Hoboken, NJ 07030, USA

ISBN-13: 978-1-5095-6315-9

A catalogue record for this book is available from the British Library.

Library of Congress Control Number: 2023951143

Typeset in 11 on 13pt Sabon
by Fakenham Prepress Solutions, Fakenham, Norfolk NR21 8NL
Printed and bound in Great Britain by CPI Group (UK) Ltd, Croydon

The publisher has used its best endeavours to ensure that the URLs for external websites referred to in this book are correct and active at the time of going to press. However, the publisher has no responsibility for the websites and can make no guarantee that a site will remain live or that the content is or will remain appropriate.

Every effort has been made to trace all copyright holders, but if any have been overlooked the publisher will be pleased to include any necessary credits in any subsequent reprint or edition.

For further information on Polity, visit our website:
politybooks.com

Contents

Acknowledgments

This book grew out of thirty-five years of friendship, conversation, and occasional collaborative writing efforts. Our thinking started during the initial months of the COVID lockdown as bitter social divisions began to emerge about our government's response to the worst public health crisis in a century. "Why can't Americans seem to agree on even the most basic government public health guidelines?" we asked ourselves – and that question set us down the road that led to this book. As we considered the issue more deeply, we started to worry. Across the world, the modern state is under attack. In the pages that follow, we try to explain why and what that means for our future.

We received a great deal of help. For their critical comments on the manuscript, we thank Dan Avnon, Sheri Berman, Michael Bernhard, Alon Burstein, Zsuzsa Csergő, Jessica Dawson, Ivan Ermakoff, Sara Goodman, Anna Grzymała-Busse, Juliet Johnson, Serhiy Kudelia, Olga Onuch, Paula Pickering, Peter Rutland, Rachel Shenhav-Goldberg, William Rosenberg, Marty Wattenberg, Dana Weinberg, Daniel Ziblatt, and participants on panels and workshops at the American Political Science Association, the Council of European Studies, the University of California, Irvine, Moldova State University, Stanford

University, and the Global Research Institute at William &
Mary. We also benefited from the perceptive feedback we
received from two anonymous reviewers who read the full
final draft of the book. Needless to say, any weaknesses
that remain are fully our own responsibility.

Our agent Larry Weissman forced us to make this book
much more accessible than it otherwise would have been,
and our editor at Polity, Louise Knight, expressed enthusiasm for the book from the get-go. We're truly grateful.

Our wives, Jennifer Stevenson and Simone Chambers,
read every word and provided invaluable feedback on the
project. Without their love and encouragement, we might
have started to write it or, more likely, we would have
thought about and endlessly talked about writing it, but
we wouldn't have finished it. We dedicate this book to
them.

1

At the Precipice

Americans love to hate the state. It's difficult now to find anyone in American politics who defends the positive contributions of "state bureaucrats" to our way of life. On the left, democratic socialists see the state as an instrument of wealthy corporate interests, while anarchists continue their quest to smash the state entirely. On the right, Christian nationalists and supporters of enhanced presidential executive power have allied to undermine the power of the secular "administrative state." Meanwhile, influential billionaires promote the staunchly anti-statist philosophy of libertarianism at think-tanks, universities, and chambers of commerce across the country.

Sometimes, hatred of the state can take fanciful forms. Silicon Valley tech mogul Peter Thiel, for example, has allied with Patri Friedman – grandson of famed libertarian economist Milton Friedman – to promote the concept of "seasteading," that is, the creation of voluntary cities on the ocean outside of any state's jurisdiction, made up of individual floating homes that can re-dock elsewhere whenever the local seasteading rules get too oppressive. And extremist groups promoting the "sovereign citizen movement," which claims that states have no legal authority over individuals whatsoever, have grown significantly since the COVID-19 pandemic. Given all of these diverse movements depicting central government as their mortal enemy, it's no wonder that belief in the existence of a global "deep state" conspiracy to stamp out human liberty is at an all-time high.[1]

But as annoying as state bureaucracies and government experts sometimes are, all of us depend on them to live what we now consider normal lives. Like the air we breathe, government agencies are mostly invisible, but without them we would be in grave danger. Without them, our food, water, and air would be poisonous, our money worthless, our children taught by incompetents or worse, our votes uncounted, and our national security violated. What if we no longer had legally constituted states, qualified experts, and well-organized bureaucracies to keep us secure, healthy, and democratic? What if we were to revert in the twenty-first century to premodern forms of personalistic rule? Not so long ago, kings, queens, royal children, grand viziers, and various hangers-on responded to public health crises, natural disasters, and questions of national security with quack remedies, consultation with oracles and soothsayers, or casting blame on "impure" outsiders. This was considered normal, and the results were horrifying: millions of needless deaths in plagues, floods, and genocides. In the modern world, a return to this sort of rule would threaten the very survival of our species. And as unlikely as it sounds, we are far closer to that precipice than most people imagine.

This is not another book about democracy's demise. It is about something far graver: the assault on the modern state itself, by both elected and unelected leaders. Some of its enemies call for the elimination of the "administrative state," the dense web of government agencies, staffed by professionals, with a degree of autonomy in deciding how laws are enacted. Others of a more conspiratorial bent see themselves engaged in a pitched battle with a shadowy "deep state." In essence, both terms have come to refer simply to the modern state as we know it – that is, central government administered according to the rule of law and staffed by employees recruited for their merit and expertise rather than due to their personal connections. This assault is part of a terrifying global trend toward resurrecting older models of state-building based on personalistic authority, one that started in Vladimir Putin's Russia but has since spread throughout the world. In countries as diverse as Hungary, Israel, the United Kingdom, and the United States, vituperative attacks on "unelected bureaucrats" have morphed into power grabs by self-aggrandizing politicians who attempt to seize control of the state for themselves and their cronies. Unfortunately, what replaces the administrative state, once it is fatally undermined, is not the free market and the flowering of personal liberty; instead, the death of government agencies organized under the rule of law inevitably brings about its only realistic political alternative: the rule of men. The logical endpoint of this trend would be a global return to a bygone era of rule by traditional sovereigns. And the threat of such an outcome is growing.

Certainly, the destruction of the impersonal state bureaucracy in the United States remains an obsession for many in the Republican Party. Former President Donald J. Trump has depicted his entire presidency as one locked in a mortal struggle with the deep state. Florida Governor Ron DeSantis enthusiastically picked up this theme in his own presidential campaign, proclaiming that "too much power has accumulated in D.C., and the result is a detached administrative state that rules over us and imposes its will on us." He put it even more bluntly to a

New Hampshire audience in summer 2023: "On bureaucracy, you know, we're going to have all these deep state people, you know, we're going to start slitting throats on day one and be ready to go." Not to be outdone by Trump or DeSantis, Arkansas Governor Sarah Huckabee Sanders tried to force all applicants to nonpartisan state board and committee jobs to write up to five hundred words on what they "admire" about her accomplishments – before flipflopping and blaming this on a "design error" in her hiring questionnaire. And Representative Marjorie Taylor Greene has gone as far as to propose a "national divorce" involving the separation of "red states and blue states" – essentially, the disintegration of the United States itself – in order to "shrink the federal government."[2]

Lest one think that such criticisms are mere flights of overheated rhetoric, it's important to emphasize that the assault on the modern state has already done a great deal of damage. Consider a revealing incident midway through the Trump presidency, when his Agriculture Secretary, Sonny Perdue, announced the relocation of the USDA's Economic Research Services and the National Institute of Food and Agriculture from Washington, DC to Kansas City, Missouri. Rather than move, about half the employees of both agencies chose to quit. This result was intentional: to wipe out the department's capacity to provide accurate information about the impact of climate change, threats to food security, and tax breaks to farmers. As one USDA official noted: "We've lost hundreds, if not thousands of staff years of expertise." Another summed up the aftermath as follows: "The agencies have been decimated. Their ability to perform the functions they were created to perform – it doesn't exist anymore." Trump advisor Steve Bannon, who had promised to "deconstruct the administrative state" (a phrase adapted, sometimes with attribution, from Vladimir Lenin), got exactly what he wanted.[3]

But this is just a small taste of what might await us in the future. Trump made it clear that one of his first acts, were he to be returned to the presidency, would be to revive "Schedule F," a drastic reduction in civil service protections for federal employees implemented in the last days of his administration. "We need to make it much easier to fire rogue bureaucrats who are deliberately undermining democracy or, at a minimum, just want to keep their jobs," Trump declared. "Congress should pass historic reforms empowering the president to ensure that any bureaucrat who is corrupt, incompetent or unnecessary for the job can be told – did you ever hear this – 'You're fired, get out, you're fired.' Have to do it. Deep state. Washington will be an entirely different place." Following Trump's lead, Governor DeSantis proposed "parceling out federal agencies to other parts of the country" as a way to "re-constitutionalize government." And the devastating implications of Representative Greene's "national divorce" for the ability of the US administrative state to carry out its essential functions can scarcely be imagined.

Much of the analysis of the Trump phenomenon has depicted the ex-president as a would-be dictator – with the implication that his supporters are implicitly antidemocratic as well. Of course, one can read the unfolding of the Trump presidency, from his dalliances with Vladimir Putin to his efforts to undermine the US legal system and hold onto power, as a story of democratic decline. Yet Trumpism is much more than this and will certainly outlast Trump himself. Whether by publicly attacking his own foreign policy and intelligence apparatus, contradicting and upstaging his leading medical specialists, or denigrating the leadership of US law enforcement agencies, Trump promoted his personal power – and that of his cronies – at the direct expense of the experts we used to trust to manage the complex challenges of the modern era. And he's not alone. When Trump and others like him promise to destroy the deep state, they are really threatening to undermine legally constituted state bureaucracies altogether.

But let's put Trump aside for a moment to think about the broader question: how, exactly, did we reach this point? To answer this question, we need to look beyond the United States. In fact, the Trump presidency was part of a larger phenomenon: a global wave of rebellion against the modern state. In countries around the world, libertarians, religious nationalists, and supporters of strong executive power have aligned against what they see as the threat to human freedom stemming from overweening state regulation. The specific nature of this coalition varies from place to place – libertarianism tends to be stronger in the more developed countries than in postcommunist regions – but in every case these groups are united in their hatred of the professionals and experts who staff government agencies and international organizations. Unfortunately, politics, like nature, abhors a vacuum: the breakdown of modern state institutions brings in its wake not "liberty" or "free markets," but rather an alternative type of political rule built on personal loyalties and connections to the ruler.

The great German sociologist Max Weber had a word for this type of rule: patrimonialism, based on the arbitrary rule of leaders who view themselves as traditional "fathers" of their nations and who run the state as a family business of sorts. Historically, patrimonial states such as the Netherlands of the sixteenth and seventeenth centuries and the tsarist Russian Empire of the eighteenth century possessed important capabilities. They extracted revenue from their people, violently put down rivals at home, sometimes permitted favored clients to get rich, and frequently invaded their neighbors. But patrimonial states had "strong thumbs" and "no fingers": they were capable of coercion and intermittent support for merchants and intellectuals, but they were simply awful at providing the predictable enforcement of laws characteristic of modern capitalism.[4]

In all these respects, patrimonialism is a very old type of government – one that most of us thought had been relegated to history. And for good reason: patrimonial regimes couldn't compete militarily or economically with states led by expert bureaucracies. Yet a series of global crises in the twenty-first century has unexpectedly made the rule of the supposedly benevolent father and his extended family newly attractive to angry, marginalized publics in countries on every continent. A slew of self-aggrandizing leaders has taken full advantage of this historical moment by seizing state assets for themselves and their loyalists, while labeling anyone who opposes them as part of the deep state. In every case, the result has been a steep decline in the state's ability to provide essential services such as health care, education, and safety.

This book will diagnose and explain the full-scale global assault on the modern state that now threatens all our futures. It shifts our focus from the decline of democracy to the rise of personalistic rule as an unexpected and dangerously attractive alternative to modern forms of civic governance. Words like *autocracy, dictatorship, authoritarianism*, and *populism* don't fully describe what the modern enemies of the state do when they come to power. We are accustomed to assuming that the advance of modernity would lead to increasingly global compliance with the rule of law. But the practice of the new "rule of men" is to ignore, sideline, or dismantle their expert agencies. These leaders staff the state with family members, friends, and sycophants, regardless of their level of incompetence. The eventual reckoning is inevitable. The bungled response to the COVID-19 pandemic, crumbling infrastructure, financial crises from unregulated banking, the erosion of safety standards for food and water, and an overheated planet all show what lies ahead. More than ever, we need to reclaim the state, defending it against those who would denigrate all government agencies as nests of self-serving bureaucrats or imagined deep state conspiracies. The alternative is unthinkable: a return to the premodern condition of most human societies, in which most people faced lives that were indeed as Thomas Hobbes once described – nasty, brutish, and short.[5]

In what follows, we focus first on the United States. How did the notion of a "deep state conspiracy," previously a fringe viewpoint held mostly on the left, become a common belief among leaders and supporters of the US Republican Party? Distrust of the central government is a longstanding American cultural trait, and a healthy skepticism about federal government overreach is of course perfectly understandable. Yet in the twenty-first century, this older form of anti-state sentiment has now morphed into something very different, namely, an explicit attempt to eviscerate the civil service and to dismantle most US central government agencies. Behind this effort, we show, is an unholy alliance of three quite different political movements: extreme libertarians, Christian nationalists, and unabashed supporters of enhanced executive power. These groups disagree about many fundamental issues. Yet they are entirely of one mind on the need to disrupt the normal functioning of the secular administrative state. Indeed, they may ultimately succeed in doing so, with disastrous future consequences for America and the world.

Paradoxically, however, this threat has mostly gone unnoticed. Instead, public debate has been overwhelmingly focused on a related, but quite different issue – namely, the uncertain future of global democracy. We criticize the nearly universal assumption that political regimes can be neatly divided into two types: democracy and authoritarianism. As important as this distinction is, it overlooks an equally important dimension of political organization: whether the state and economy are governed primarily according to laws and procedures applied without regard to personal backgrounds, or instead by personal connections and loyalty to particular leaders. This second dimension does not always coincide with the first. In addition to rule-of-law democracies and personalistic autocracies, there are also many electoral democracies in which power and wealth are primarily distributed through personal networks, such as the Philippines, as well as authoritarian regimes which have historically ruled primarily through the firm application of laws and procedures, like the German Empire in the nineteenth century or Singapore in the twentieth century.

We argue that the "democracy versus authoritarianism" debate has blinded us to an even more important contemporary political threat: the global spread of patrimonial regimes – that is, regimes in which leaders posing as the "father" of the nation demand unquestioned personal loyalty and treat the state like a family business. Around the world, the hard-won professional expertise of state agencies – the very core of modern governance – is being replaced by nepotism, cronyism, and partisan conformity as the basis for political appointments. It is no exaggeration to say that the outcome of this struggle will determine the fate of the modern state itself.

This unexpected global assault on the modern state and the return of a premodern rule of men cries out for explanation. Why now? Where did it come from? While the intellectual antecedents of libertarianism, religious nationalism, and so-called unitary executive theory date back several decades, the global assault on the modern state fully crystallized only after Vladimir Putin succeeded in building a powerful patrimonial regime in post-Soviet Russia. Donald Trump's consistently obsequious behavior toward Putin has long puzzled political observers. But the exact nature of the link between the two men is difficult to investigate without triggering a chorus of criticisms about resurrecting what Trump liked to call the "Russia hoax." Clearly, Putin did not call Trump on a regular basis to give him orders. We can, however, document a different sort of bond between them: namely, that they represent different manifestations of the contemporary assault on the modern state. In fact, Putin's resurrection of tsarist imperialism in Russia after the collapse of the Soviet Union served as the original model for other would-be patrimonial leaders around the world over the past two decades. Social conditions in post-Soviet Russia – characterized by accelerating socioeconomic inequality, inefficient rust-belt industries employing millions of blue-collar workers, and traditional rural communities unprepared for globalization – appear in retrospect to be quite similar to those facing developing countries and advanced capitalist powers alike after the 2008 financial crisis. Putin's successful mobilization in Russia of mass anger at "corrupt elites" who "betrayed the nation," his portrayal of Western global institutions as bent on the destruction of Russia's traditional cultural values, and his promotion of strong personalistic rule as an alternative, unexpectedly turned out to resonate far beyond the post-Soviet context.

The "out of Russia" part of our story, we realize, may be met with skepticism. Is Putin's establishment of a new tsarist state in Russia really connected to anti-state movements in the developed West? To this objection we can offer two rejoinders, one historical and the other political. Historically, political innovations, both the "good" and "bad," have emerged in the most unlikely places, on the peripheries of the global order. Who would have ever thought that liberal democracy would emerge in England, an island on the edge of the Roman empire with bad weather, bland food, and a nobility that liked nothing better than hunting with dogs? And yet it happened. Our second rejoinder is related to the first. We wonder whether hesitancy to accept Russia as a source of political innovation – even innovation we may find distasteful – reflects a degree of political parochialism and perhaps even ethnocentrism. It is worth recalling that a different alternative order that changed the world – Leninism – also emerged from Russia just over a century ago. Of course, once the modern version of the rule of the good father established a foothold in other locations, the process of its spread became more complex and multifaceted; it jumped from country to country, back and forth, as would-be patrimonial rulers learned from each other. But the global assault on the modern state started, we maintain, in Russia.[6]

Putin's model of patrimonial rule spread throughout the world in part because of the Kremlin's direct promotion of pro-Russian parties and leaders – little Putins or at least Putin admirers – on a global scale. But an equally important driver of this return to the rule of men has been domestic conditions that made personalistic rule appealing in a broad range of countries. The diffusion of patrimonial rule began in the former Soviet Union, in countries like Kazakhstan, Belarus, and Ukraine before the Euromaidan revolution, where modern state institutions had always been weak. In these cases, Putin's foreign policy served to reinforce preexisting political realities. But the patrimonial wave later spread to Hungary and Poland, where the European Union had spent fifteen years closely monitoring budding Western-style civil services and judiciaries. From there it moved further afield, to unexpected countries such as Israel, where Prime Minister Benjamin Netanyahu pivoted from a previous strict adherence to the rule of law to attacking his own judiciary and police. Most shockingly, however, the assault on modern government took root in Boris Johnson's United Kingdom and the United States under Donald Trump, where both leaders went about building their personal rule and attacking their own states' integrity and capacity. Ultimately, the global patrimonial wave generated strange new geopolitical alliances, not only among leaders like Putin, Orbán, Netanyahu, and Trump, but also between these men and like-minded strongmen in the less-developed countries such as Recep Tayyip Erdoğan in Turkey, Narendra Modi in India, and Jair Bolsonaro in Brazil. The assault on the state appeared in divergent forms from country to country, as leaders drew on different grievances and traditions. But in each case, the result was the same: a stark challenge to modern governance based on the rule of law.

What can be done to reverse the assault on the modern state that now threatens all our futures? We propose a four-part strategy. The first task is to raise awareness of the problem, which has thus far been misunderstood as a struggle to defend democracy against authoritarianism – a framing that blinds us to the ways in which the attack on modern state agencies can unfold in democratic and autocratic countries alike. The politically active public needs to be fully cognizant of the key warning signs that indicate the erosion of modern state governance: the promotion of the ruler's family and cronies to politically powerful positions, direct attacks on the staff of state agencies and the independence of judiciaries, and the denigration of professional expertise as a criterion for political promotion in favor of loyalty tests. Second, we should fortify and honor the modern state rather than attack it. Although much of our book describes the assault on the state from the right, saving the state will also require resisting siren calls of the left. These include recommendations ranging from the radical democratic inclusion of ordinary citizens into everyday state administration to the rejection of meritocracy as a principle for recruitment into educational, cultural, and bureaucratic institutions. Such well-intentioned cures will be ineffective and quite possibly worse than the disease itself. Third, there needs to be an urgent drive to recruit the next generation of young people to commit themselves to lives of government service, lest the worsening attrition of professional expertise in our state agencies pass the tipping point. Fourth, our foreign policy must also meet the challenge. We need to recognize that the assault on the modern state is being explicitly encouraged by patrimonial rulers who would love nothing more than to dismantle the global liberal order.

In this context, Russia's war on Ukraine is much more than a land grab. It constitutes an attempt to create a bloc of like-minded patrimonial rulers on the European landmass. Beyond Europe, the growing challenge of a Chinese regime that itself increasingly displays patrimonial features can only be met by an international coalition capable of defending the legal framework that undergirds individual human rights and free markets. The future of humanity depends, more profoundly than ever, on an alliance of law-based states committed to a world governed by shared rules, rather than a view of international politics as relations among big men.

Much ink has been spilled on the threat of democratic erosion, and we share that concern. But defending the modern state is also vital for preserving democracy. From protecting civil rights to simply counting the votes, it's hard to imagine a stable democratic future without the machinery of modern government. In its absence, elected representatives of the people may pull the formal levers of power – but these levers are increasingly unlikely to be attached to anything. The world has survived past periods of democratic crisis, but in a time of mounting social and environmental threats, it is unlikely to survive a return of the rule of men.

2

The Deep State Bogeyman

Patrick Byrne isn't the sort of person one would have expected to become an avid conspiracy theorist. Son of John Byrne, the famed CEO who built GEICO into one of the world's largest insurance companies, Patrick was educated at some of the best universities in the world, with an undergraduate degree from Dartmouth, a master's degree as a Marshall Scholar at Cambridge University, and a PhD in philosophy from Stanford. Byrne then followed in his father's footsteps as a highly successful CEO in his own right, turning Overstock.com into one of the early avatars of online shopping. Brilliant, successful, rich, with rugged good looks, Byrne was seemingly on track for a prominent place in the establishment.

Instead, Byrne became a tireless purveyor of attacks on the deep state. An early interest in libertarian philosophy, combined with bad personal experiences with major US banks when short sellers were targeting his company, convinced him over time that Wall Street and the mainstream media were working together behind the scenes to control hidden financial information. The only way out of their clutches, Byrne told rapt audiences at prominent libertarian conventions, was to build an entirely new economy on cryptocurrency.

After one such lecture in 2015, Byrne was approached by a fawning young Russian audience member – Maria Butina, later convicted of spying for Russia. He reported their love affair to the FBI: "Maria's pillow talk became less about John Locke and John Stuart Mill, and more about the US political circles in which she was coming to swank around." But his suspicions grew when, as he claims, the Feds didn't do anything to stop Butina's subsequent meetings and liaisons with prominent Republicans. Ultimately, Byrne became convinced that the US intelligence agencies were part of an even bigger deep state conspiracy.[1]

Since then, Byrne has devoted much of his fortune, and most of his time, to disseminating propaganda against the COVID-19 vaccine, lobbying for private school voucher programs, and repeating falsehoods about the "rigging" of Dominion Voting Systems' election machines. Byrne's self-produced movie *The Deep Rig* advances well-worn myths about how the 2020 US presidential election was "stolen" from Donald Trump, complete with appearances by fellow pro-Trump conspiracy theorists like retired General Michael Flynn and retired Colonel Phil Waldron. The film's tag line, "How the political hysteria of a nation allowed for unprecedented election fraud," sums up Byrne's political evolution. On December 18, 2020 – just four days after Joe Biden was officially named president-elect – Byrne, Flynn, and like-minded attorney Sidney Powell even managed to meet with Trump in the Oval Office to share their "unhinged" views of the presidential election, before more senior White House aides could intervene.[2]

All of this raises an important question: just how do smart, successful people like Patrick Byrne become convinced that there is a deep state? Part of the answer is that politics does often seem mysterious and complex. It sometimes feels as if our understanding of political life barely scratches the surface. What is the underlying structure of power? Are we missing some sort of crucial backstory, some sort of special knowledge that will reveal otherwise hidden or obscure connections between people and events? Who is pulling the strings? It's a fair question to ask because, like it or not, political power affects our lives in profound ways – determining war and peace, health and sickness, wealth and poverty, and the quality and extent of our lives.

But there are hazards to thinking about politics this way. The search for "hidden forces" that somehow manipulate political outcomes can quickly produce a culture of generalized suspicion. As any regular viewer of Fox News or devotee of talk radio can tell you, the idea that a deep state conspiracy threatens individual liberty and the American way of life is a constant theme in the US conservative media today. A whole spate of books has appeared in recent years amplifying this theme, with terrifying titles like *Killing the Deep State: The War to Save President Trump*, *The Deep State: How an Army of Bureaucrats Protected Barack Obama and Is Working to Destroy the Trump Agenda*, and *The Deeper State: Inside the War on Trump by Corrupt Elites, Secret Societies, and the Builders of an Imminent Final Empire*. Consumers of these dubious sources of information are told that the conspiracy behind this supposed shadow government is indeed a vast one. Apparently, it includes not only the "unelected government bureaucrats" themselves, but also their allies in federal law enforcement and the military, "cultural Marxists" at US universities, supporters of LGBTQ+ rights, international banking and financial elites such as George Soros, and other "globalists" who hate America – to name just a few of the usual targets.[3]

For those Americans who primarily get their news from conservative media, the incessant repetition of these dark themes is certainly having an effect. Public opinion polls show that almost 40 percent of Americans believe that the deep state worked to overthrow President Trump, with strong majorities of both Republicans and Fox News viewers in agreement with this statement. And nearly half of Americans accept the basic idea that a shadowy group of military, intelligence, and other government officials somehow secretly directs national policy.[4]

Clearly something is terribly wrong with the state of American political discourse. Given that so many US citizens appear convinced that their destinies are being controlled behind the scenes by hidden, evil forces, it's not surprising that trust in government – along with trust in one's fellow citizens – has fallen to historic lows. The pervasive feeling of powerlessness that deep state rhetoric engenders in its audience can quickly morph into seething, generalized anger at all established institutions and the elites who manage them. The events of January 6, 2021, provide a graphic illustration of just how grave a threat the republic now faces as a result.[5]

But where did this notion of the deep state come from? Conservatives in the US might be surprised to learn that the phrase itself originated not on the political right, but, rather, among protesters, leftwing activists, and Islamists in Turkey during the 1990s. And in the Turkish context, the concept of the deep state – the *derin devlet* – actually made a lot of sense. After all, ever since the establishment of the Turkish Republic by Kemal Ataturk in 1923 as a secular, modernizing state, the Turkish military had repeatedly intervened to short-circuit democratic politics whenever it appeared that Marxist, Islamist, or Kurdish separatist movements might threaten the regime. Turkey experienced three military coups between 1960 and 1980, each time preventing the formation of a truly representative parliamentary government. The regime also relied on shadowy alliances with underground criminals who used violence to suppress opposition journalists and labor activists, while giving politicians in parliament "plausible deniability."[6]

An unexpected car crash revealed this sordid arrangement to the Turkish public. In November 1996, a truck plowed into a Mercedes in Susurluk, a provincial town southeast of Istanbul, killing three of its four passengers. Naturally, the names of the victims made it into police reports – at which point things got very strange. The passengers in the Mercedes, as it turned out, included not only a former deputy captain of an elite government antiterrorist squad and a centrist member of the Turkish parliament (the lone survivor), but also the notorious criminal Abdullah Çatlı and his girlfriend. Çatlı was wanted by Interpol after escaping from a Swiss prison where he was being held on drug-trafficking charges. He was a known associate of the notorious hitman Mehmet Ali Ağca, who in 1978 had attempted to assassinate Pope John Paul II. So, what were Çatlı and his girlfriend doing in a fancy car with a high-ranking police officer and politician? Why did investigators find a collection of government-issued pistols and rifles in the trunk of the vehicle? And why on earth was Çatlı carrying a number of fake identity documents – signed personally by the Turkish minister of the interior?

Clearly, there was a real conspiracy between the Turkish political establishment and the criminal underworld at work. Unfortunately, despite the weeks of grassroots protests that erupted after the Susurluk scandal, no transparent official account of the affair was ever released, and no indictments for wrongdoing were ever issued. A year later, the Turkish military decided to intervene in parliamentary politics once again, this time to oust the newly installed Islamist Prime Minister Necmettin Erbakan in favor of a secular government. Since the military now chose to exercise its power only behind the scenes of the democratic façade, rather than establishing a military government, Turkish observers termed this a "postmodern coup." Erbakan and his Islamist party were banned, and Erbakan himself was later charged with corruption and sentenced to prison. It's hardly surprising that President Recep Tayyip Erdoğan, Erbakan's direct political heir, lived in constant fear of real or imagined conspiracies to bring down his government. Nor is it a surprise that he blamed these on the continuing influence of the Turkish deep state.[7]

What *is* surprising is that over the past quarter century, the idea of the deep state somehow spread from the Turkish context, with its specific history of hidden political alliances to undermine democratic politics, to countries around the world with highly diverse political systems. How did this transformation take place?

For the first decade after the Susurluk scandal, the concept of the deep state was taken up primarily by journalists and academics focusing on the Middle East, who explored forms of "shadow power" in other countries in Turkey's neighborhood. Egypt, for example, could also easily be depicted as a regime in which true power was exercised by the military behind the scenes, regardless of the results of parliamentary elections – and analysis of the "Egyptian deep state" has become something of a cottage industry. Beyond the context of military regimes, Islamist and one-party dictatorships such as Iran and Syria could also be analyzed in similar terms as countries ruled by shadowy networks of intelligence agents and their civilian enforcers. By the 2010s, the concept of the deep state was widespread in the field of Middle East studies, and among educated publics in many countries.[8]

But the spread of the idea of the deep state did not stop at the boundaries of the Middle East. Instead, it was increasingly taken up by leftwing academics and journalists, who expanded it to shine a light on what these authors considered to be similar forms of hidden power in advanced capitalist countries – including the United States. Marxist theory teaches that capitalist "democracy" is just a smokescreen to disguise the perpetuation of the profits and control of the global bourgeoisie. Behind the scenes, this argument goes, wealthy elites continue to pressure politicians in every major political party to cut taxes, eliminate regulations, and repress labor activism. In this sense, the idea that there is always a hidden deep state operating under the surface of democratic elections fits quite well with radical political theory. Authors writing on the role of the deep state in the 2000s and early 2010s tended to focus on the growing power of the US military–industrial complex, intelligence agencies surveilling the American population, "big oil," and the international financial elite. None of this analysis – some of which is entirely sensible, and some of which veers off into crackpot conspiracy theorizing – had much impact on mainstream American political discourse before 2016. With the emergence of Donald J. Trump as a serious candidate for the Republican nomination for the US presidential elections, however, the concept of the deep state took on a brand-new meaning.[9]

The appeal of conspiracy theories is the same as for all theories (even nonconspiratorial ones): they appear to explain a lot with a little. But what makes a conspiracy theory distinctive – what makes it a *conspiracy* theory – is its focus on hidden power. Like the far left, the alt-right had its own theory about the sources of hidden power in America – and it spilled forth in the first weeks of Trump's presidency, as some of his first executive orders implementing what became known as the "Muslim ban" were thwarted by judges and career civil servants who questioned their legality. Trump's supporters were aghast. Why was

21

the new president of the United States immediately facing so much internal resistance to the implementation of one of his central campaign promises? To explain how this could happen, the anonymous author, "Virgil" of *Breitbart News*, depicted hidden forces consisting of "the complex of bureaucrats, technocrats, and plutocrats that likes things just the way they are and wants to keep them like that – elections be damned," who were engaging in a "great power struggle" with the new president. Through defamation, leaks, slow-walking or opposing executive orders, Virgil maintained, the deep state was actively thwarting the will of the people.[10]

Much less anonymous was former Speaker of the House and Trump ally Newt Gingrich who, when asked why Trump was facing so much early resistance, replied bluntly: "Of course, the deep state exists. There's a permanent state of massive bureaucracies that do whatever they want and set up deliberate leaks to attack the president." Although Trump himself held off using the term "deep state" until November 2017, his closest advisors fed him a steady diet of tales of secret opposition and resistance emanating from within the establishment – Obama holdovers, career civil servants in the National Security Council, journalists in the mainstream media, and "globalists" everywhere. It worked. According to one count, Trump invoked the deep state at least a dozen times in 2018 and nearly twice as often the following year. He was joined by a chorus of rightwing commentators, journalists, and political appointees who warned of sabotage in virtually every branch of the government. In time, the notion of a deep state conspiracy became commonplace in American conservative circles.[11]

Of course, all good conspiracy theories have a tinge of truth. That's what makes them plausible and powerful. Some of what Trump proposed early on – including the executive order banning citizens of predominantly Muslim states from entering the United States – did elicit opposition from government agencies. Responding to Trump's claim that his inaugural crowd was larger than Obama's, the National Park Service faithfully reported its lower, and more accurate, estimate of the crowd size. It had no choice. The American state has been carefully built up over an extended period of time through a series of important legislative acts and judicial decisions that no president could by fiat render null and void. The fact that the president had only limited power over his own bureaucracy obviously surprised Trump himself, but it also brought to public consciousness the much broader question of the proper role of the "administrative state" – a term that for many Americans simply sounds like an arcane version of the "deep state." In fact, the administrative state refers to the powers delegated by Congress to departments and agencies to implement the laws it passes (usually with regulations and rulemaking). But to the uninitiated, deep state versus administrative state may sound like a distinction without a difference.[12]

Nobody understood this better than former Breitbart News executive chair, Trump campaign chief, and senior White House advisor Stephen K. Bannon. Bannon would later declare that the "deep state conspiracy theory is for nut cases ... America isn't Turkey or Egypt ... there's nothing 'deep' about it." But in the first weeks of Trump's presidency, he did little to downplay its existence. Instead, Bannon played on anxieties about the deep state as a bridge of sorts to the conservative establishment. In a February 2017 appearance at the Conservative Political Action Committee, Bannon described three goals for the new administration – national security, "economic nationalism," and the "deconstruction of the administrative state." This last, seemingly obscure, phrase garnered loud applause from the audience. Conservatives had long bridled at the powers of bureaucratic regulation that Congress had delegated to federal departments and agencies, seeing these powers as an attack on individual liberty. Bannon vaguely alluded to plans for presidential intervention or perhaps simply letting these agencies die on the vine through neglect. Some of this rhetoric might have been consistent with traditional Republican talking points, but Bannon had something quite different in mind, something that he considered far more revolutionary: to target and unravel the machinery of modern government itself.[13]

With the metastasizing of the notion of a hidden deep state from a sensible depiction of the workings of Turkey's military-led regime in the 1990s, to a generalized critique of the global power of the military–industrial complex, to a conspiracy theory that the entire modern adminis-trative state is secretly organized to thwart the popular will, the term has begun to poison political discourse on a truly global scale. In Israel, Prime Minister Benjamin Netanyahu and his supporters began to echo Trump's usage of the deep state concept to disparage the Israeli judiciary and law enforcement as they prepared to indict him on corruption charges. Cronies of Prime Minister Viktor Orbán in Hungary curried favor with American pro-Trump conservatives by depicting Orbán as a fearless fighter against the "deep state of Brussels." In the summer of 2022, British Prime Minister Boris Johnson, struggling to keep his position after revolts within his own Tory Party parliamentary faction, warned that the "deep state" was trying to reverse Brexit and "haul us back into alignment with the EU as a prelude to our eventual return." Even former National Security Agency contractor Edward Snowden, from his refuge in Russia, has embraced the new conflation of the deep state and the "administrative state," claiming in an interview with Italian journalists: "now the deep state is not just the intelligence agencies, it is really a way of referring to the career bureaucracy of government. There are officials who sit in powerful positions, who don't leave when presidents do, who watch presidents come and go, they influence policy, they influence presidents and say: this is what we have always done, this is what we must do, and if you don't do this, people will die."[14]

Still, the mass appeal of the idea of the deep state remains mysterious. Why do so many politicians and voters, even in the richest and most developed countries in the world, now embrace a viewpoint that would have been relegated to the fringes of the political spectrum not so long ago?

What makes the deep state such an attractive political slogan is precisely its all-encompassing nature. Now that the deep state has become a synonym for the modern administrative state, opponents of state bureaucracy from diverse political camps can all join the chorus in attacking it. We have already seen how the concept resonates for leftwing critics of liberal capitalism and the "surveillance state," due to its overlap with older Marxist notions of the state as nothing more than the instrument of the "ruling class." Snowden's comments fit within this general pattern. But how did the deep state become the primary bogeyman of the conservative right as well as the far left? To understand this, we need to look more closely at the embrace of the concept by three otherwise diverse groupings allied with the US Republican Party – extreme libertarians, Christian nationalists, and supporters of expanded executive power. For all three of these factions, the total destruction of the modern administrative state is an inspiring ideal – albeit for completely different reasons. Their common loathing of what they see as the deep state has allowed them to forge an unholy alliance that now threatens to destroy effective government altogether.

* * *

The modern libertarian movement traces its origins back to two primary intellectual sources: the "Objectivist" philosophy of Ayn Rand and the early writings of the economists of the so-called Austrian School – in particular, Ludwig von Mises and his mentee Friedrich Hayek. To this day, libertarian organizations and philanthropic foundations continue to promote the distribution of their "sacred texts" – in particular, Rand's novel *Atlas Shrugged* and Hayek's antisocialist treatise *The Road to Serfdom*.[15]

To be sure, there are differences between Rand's and Hayek's worldviews, and the relationship among adherents of their views and contemporary libertarian politics is complex. Rand was an émigré from the Soviet Union whose family lost all their property in the Bolshevik Revolution. Heavily influenced by the philosophy of Friedrich Nietzsche, Rand argued for capitalism as an arena in which heroic men who rejected all forms of social conformity could achieve greatness solely through their personal efforts. The success of her novel *The Fountainhead*, published in 1943, which chronicled the challenges and triumphs of her protagonist, the iconoclastic architect Howard Roark, gave her a devoted following among would-be heroic individualists. By the 1950s, a circle of genuine true believers in Rand's philosophy – including a young Alan Greenspan, later Chair of the Federal Reserve – regularly met in her New York apartment to hear her brilliant thoughts. Rand gave the group the ironic name "The Collective." By the time she published what she considered her greatest novel *Atlas Shrugged*, in 1957, Rand had become a well-known public intellectual with a global audience. As happens in many personality cults, however, Rand's group repeatedly split into warring factions. A particularly bitter schism was spurred on by her secret love affair in the 1950s with her deputy in the Objectivist movement, Nathan Branden, known only to their respective spouses. When

Branden refused to resume the affair in the 1960s – he had by then taken up with a young fashion model whom he later married – Rand bitterly denounced him, and he was ostracized from the group. Rand also personally hated the term "libertarianism." She accused leading figures of the libertarian movement of stealing her ideas and excommunicated anyone who associated too closely with it. Nevertheless, a significant number of former Objectivists who had been personally rejected by Rand continued to promote and disseminate her teachings within the growing libertarian movement in the 1970s and 1980s.[16]

Von Mises and Hayek arrived in the United States from their native Austria as professors of economics who had long been involved in polemical debates against supporters of socialism and state planning. Von Mises was famous for his demonstration of the "calculation problem" under state socialism – namely, that in the absence of free markets, there would be no way for state planners to figure out how to set the proper prices for capital, labor, or goods. Hayek took Von Mises's insight further to argue that all forms of state intervention in the workings of the market would necessarily generate inefficiency and threats to individual liberty – views he expressed most forcefully in his 1944 book *The Road to Serfdom*, which gained a mass audience with the publication a year later of an abridged version in *Readers' Digest* and a picture book version in *Look* magazine (the latter broadly distributed as a pamphlet by General Motors).

These ideas found fertile soil in a post-World War II America beginning to come to grips with the scale of human destruction wrought by National Socialist totalitarianism in Germany, and the need for long-term vigilance against another totalitarian system based on Marxist-Leninist socialism in the Soviet Union. In this context, both Rand's Objectivism and the anti-statism of the Austrian School appeared prophetic about the tyrannical nature of these forms of dictatorial "socialism," and an excellent philosophical foundation for defending the American free-market alternative. To be sure, anti-communism was far from the only topic of intellectual interest to these thinkers, and they disagreed about many other issues. Yet Objectivism and Hayekianism are fully united in two core beliefs: that the state, left unchecked, will always seek to expand its power and influence over individuals, and that allowing the state to intervene directly in capitalist markets is a slippery slope to tyranny. Given these precepts, it is not hard to see why adherents of Rand's and Hayek's worldviews would share a sense that the rapid growth of the administrative state in the postwar period – including an increase in United States government spending from 3 percent of GDP in 1929 to over 31 percent of GDP in 2020 – poses a major threat to freedom.[17]

It was also predictable that the works of Rand, von Mises, and Hayek would appeal in particular to wealthy capitalist CEOs with a philosophical streak such as Charles and David Koch. Despite careful new research about the role of "dark money" distributed by the Koch brothers to conservative politicians, academics, and activists over the past several decades, the sincerity of their theoretical commitments has been generally underestimated. The young David Koch encountered Rand's novels as a student at MIT in the 1950s, and he returned to read her books in greater depth in the 1970s when he became more involved in philanthropy. In 1980, he ran for the post of vice president of the United States on the ticket of the US Libertarian Party – competing not only with President Jimmy Carter, but also the eventual victor Ronald Reagan – and received around 1 percent of the popular vote. For his part, Charles Koch often cited von Mises's 1949 treatise *Human Action* as a major philosophical influence. Even after the death of David Koch in 2019, influential libertarian-conservative think-tanks and academic centers such as the Cato Institute, the Heritage Foundation, and the Mercatus Center at George Mason University continued to rely on large donations from the Koch family.[18]

Libertarian philosophy has also proven to be remarkably attractive to another group of billionaires who imagine themselves to be heroic disrupters of the status quo: tech moguls whose startup companies in Silicon Valley have grown into massive profit centers. Some of them envision a future in which those who master advanced technology will create entirely new forms of social order that will make the state obsolete. Others simply work to undermine government regulations that might limit their corporate control over our personal information. Whatever their mix of motivations, CEOs such as Peter Thiel and Mark Zuckerberg have openly declared their support for libertarian principles, using their vast wealth to promote lobbyists and politicians who share their disdain for government bureaucrats. In line with his mercurial nature, Elon Musk eschews any consistent label for his political beliefs, but he too declares that, "in general, I believe government should rarely impose its will upon the people." Many tech moguls, it is true, still tend to support candidates from the Democratic Party – but a study by political scientists at Stanford has found that they differ from mainstream Democrats on two key issues: they strongly oppose both government regulation and labor unions.[19]

Libertarians are surely correct to warn that past a certain point, state control over economic life poses a real threat to individual liberty. The rise and fall of the Soviet Union, and its devastating economic aftermath, demonstrated clearly that a single system of central economic planning – even if capable of successfully mobilizing breakneck industrialization for a time, as Stalin did in the 1930s and '40s – is eventually bound to run aground owing to the inherent inefficiency and irrationality of trying to determine uniform production, consumption, and distribution decisions for an entire population. For this reason, except in the "hermit kingdom" of North Korea, every Leninist regime that survived the Soviet collapse in 1991 – China, Laos, Vietnam, and Cuba – has since reintroduced markets to a greater or lesser degree.

But it hardly follows from this observation that the only sort of state consistent with the preservation of individual rights is a minimalist "nightwatchman" state that limits itself to the preservation of safety, security, and property – and nothing more. History has also shown clearly that the "slope" from pure laissez-faire capitalism to state socialist tyranny is anything but slippery. In fact, all sorts of intermediate levels of state ownership of property, state economic planning, and welfare state redistribution of income are possible within democratic political systems. Remarkably, notwithstanding Hayek's warnings in *The Road to Serfdom*, not a single country with a reformist social democratic government has *ever* "slid" into one-party tyranny. Instead, socialist dictatorships typically come to power through revolutions against the existing democratic capitalist order, as socialist dictators are proud to proclaim. We should therefore be able to argue that the state still has an important role to play in modern democratic capitalist countries without worrying that, even by broaching the topic, we are somehow inviting the imminent destruction of individual liberty.

Unfortunately, the powerful influence of libertarian thinking in American politics and culture today has gravely undermined public debate about just what level of state bureaucracy we might wish to maintain, and at what cost in taxation and regulation – a subject about which reasonable people can disagree and, ultimately, compromise. In place of a productive discussion about how citizens of a democratic polity might strike a balance between overly invasive state intervention in their lives, on the one hand, and insufficient state provision of public goods, on the other, libertarian thinking has inspired a massive crusade against state bureaucracy itself. The result is that it is not only leftwing radicals worried about government surveillance and the power of the military–industrial complex, but also mainstream pro-market conservatives who have become increasingly convinced that something like the deep state really does possess a hidden power to control our lives.

* * *

Libertarians may be natural candidates for deep state conspiracy theories. But for Christian nationalists, the attraction is less obvious. Even so, the Christian right has regularly invoked the term to describe their enemies who are supposedly working behind the scenes. At a rally in Washington, DC, on December 12, 2020, organized by the new Christian right group "the Jericho March" in the wake of President Trump's electoral defeat, retired General Michael Flynn – Trump's former national security advisor who pleaded guilty to lying to federal investigators, and ultimately the recipient of a presidential pardon – likened the walls of Jericho to those of the modern deep state and promised "we're going to knock those walls down." Another Trump advisor, Roger Stone, who had claimed to have been born again after being convicted for obstruction of justice in the Mueller investigation, told the crowd in a recorded message: "It was Jesus Christ who gave our President, Donald Trump, the courage and the compassion to save my life when I was unfairly and illegally targeted in the Mueller witch hunt ... My faith is in Jesus Christ, and we will make America great again and we will stop the steal." Radio host and conspiracy theorist Alex Jones also made an appearance, maintaining that "Christ's crucifixion was not our defeat, it was our greatest victory ... The state has no jurisdiction over any of us. Our relationship with God is sacred and is eternal." For our purposes, what is more interesting than Mike Flynn's, Roger Stone's, or Alex Jones's almost certainly insincere reliance on Christian themes and imagery to prevent the peaceful transfer of power is that they all draw on an established tradition in American Christian nationalism: the belief that a hidden power within the state, a state-within-the-state, is aiming to thwart God's will.[20]

What exactly is Christian nationalism and why would its adherents see within the modern state a conspiracy to undermine their community? Sociologists Philip Gorski and Samuel Perry summarize what they term "white Christian nationalism" with three words: freedom, order, and violence. Freedom is understood primarily as freedom from all restrictions – especially from government – for Christians to practice their religion. Order means hierarchy with white Christian men at the top. And violence is the means reserved for white Christian men to defend freedom and maintain order. These three elements of white Christian nationalism have evolved over time, but in the American variant it has tended in a clearly anti-statist direction. The reasons for this are illuminating.[21]

Like libertarians, Christian nationalists fear "socialism," but what they mean by socialism is different. Less concerned with economic redistribution from the "rich" to the "poor" or from "capital" to "labor," and the threats this might pose to individual liberty for all, white Christian nationalists worry about redistribution from the ethnically advantaged to the disadvantaged, welfare transfers not between classes but between races. The argument has a certain twisted logic. Throughout the developed West over the past five decades, leftwing critics of capitalism have become increasingly frustrated with the "working class," which seems uninterested in fundamental social change and can all too easily be divided and mobilized politically along ethnic lines. Instead, prominent figures on the progressive left have found a surrogate proletariat of sorts in the racially and ethnically disadvantaged: if the workers don't want a revolution or radical change, or even social democracy, perhaps marginalized nonwhite populations will. While such revolutionary voices hardly determine government policy, they are continuously amplified by Christian nationalist leaders to drum up outrage among their followers. And since governments and parties of the left today do draw disproportionate support from the racially and ethnically disadvantaged, they are naturally inclined to pursue policies designed to ensure greater social equality.

The state, in turn, has been the key player in leveling the playing field between dominant groups and disadvantaged minorities – in the United States, given the legacies of slavery, between White people and Black people in particular. But for this reason, Christian nationalists who wish to preserve their ethnic group's historic advantages – America's "whiteness" – frequently speak of religious and economic freedom from the government almost in the same breath. The government, they maintain, should refrain from interfering in the free market *and* from correcting past or present racial and ethnic injustices. Public authority shorn of ethnocultural advantage is of little value. Protecting freedom means preserving it for a very narrowly defined "us." Modern states that administer welfare programs, provide aid to refugees, enforce economic and environmental regulations, or devise public health and vaccine requirements are populated by "experts" who show little deference to traditional hierarchies or sources of authority. For many Christian nationalists, the state is also seen as complicit in the "great replacement," itself a conspiracy theory about the supposed desire of Jews and other "globalists" to engineer mass migration of nonwhite people to the United States and other "Western" countries to replace whites with pliant and racially inferior peoples. In Christian nationalist circles, then, it is easy to depict the deep state as an implacable enemy.

If Christian nationalists fear diminished racial and ethnic advantage, what they fear even more is the demise of traditional gender relations and the extension of rights to sexual minorities. The restoration of traditional morality with heterosexual men at the top lies at the core of their worldview. Fear of LGBTQ+ and transgender activists who might subvert this old order is a pervasive and passionate theme among right-wing Christians in America. But this particular theme has proven to be a potent one far beyond the United States. Addressing the Conservative Political Action Committee in 2022, Christian nationalist Hungarian Prime Minister Viktor Orbán proclaimed before his approving American audience: "Hungary shall protect the institution of marriage as the union of one man and one woman. Family ties shall be based on marriage or the relationship between parent and children. To sum up, the mother is a woman, the father is a man, and leave our kids alone. Full stop. End of discussion!" For his part, Russia's President Vladimir Putin has compared gender nonconformity and trans rights to the "new strains" of a "pandemic." Christian nationalist leaders throughout the world have denounced "gender ideology" and have worked diligently to restore older hierarchies and rules. But in legally oriented states with independent judiciaries, they still confront determined and highly trained judges and officials who do not easily bend to the will of elected traditionalists. Court rulings that, until quite recently, tended to limit expressions of Christianity in the public square and the ability of Christian businesses to deny service to LGBTQ+ customers have infuriated rightwing Christian activists and voters. This has turned the American judiciary itself into a major target of attacks on the deep state.[22]

In the United States, the convergence of the libertarian and Christian nationalist strands of anti-statism is most powerfully represented by the Federalist Society. Supported by hundreds of millions of dollars in private donations, it has focused its energies on restaffing the United States judiciary at all levels, in the hopes of removing impediments to the restoration of the "constitutional order" underpinned by the "free market" and ethnoreligious traditionalism. The Federalist Society's longtime leader Leonard Leo reportedly believes that "most of the New Deal and administrative state are unconstitutional, that corporations have free speech and free religion rights, that women and LGBT people are not 'protected classes' under constitutional law, and that there is no right to privacy implied by the due process clause of the Constitution (i.e., banning abortion, contraception, and gay marriage are entirely constitutional)." Judging by the rapidly changing ideological composition of the US Supreme Court, the Federalist Society's efforts have been largely successful. But for many Christian nationalists, the change has come all too slowly. Their temptation therefore is to see the continued (though eroding) separation of church and state, ongoing resistance to violations of gender and sexual equality, and the survival of the vast regulatory apparatus of federal, state, and local government agencies as the work of a secretive and hidden deep state that subverts the power of the "authentic" people.[23]

* * *

Our tour of the main political forces in the United States that now promote and disseminate the deep state conspiracy theory would not be complete without examination of a third major strain in contemporary Republican circles, one that overlaps with the libertarian and Christian nationalist camps only in part: namely, unabashed promoters of almost unlimited executive power exercised by the president. Its adherents are just as angry at the continuing power of the administrative state as libertarians and Christian nationalists, but for an even simpler reason: the ability of state agencies and judges to resist executive power blocks the power of the president to enact their favored conservative policies.

For most of the history of the United States, neither of America's major political parties supported the idea of unfettered presidential power. Wartime presidents such as Abraham Lincoln and Franklin Delano Roosevelt officially suspended ordinary constitutional limitations on executive authority, to be sure, but both did so explicitly as a response to emergency circumstances, not as the assertion of a general principle. Particularly after the adoption of the Twenty-Second Amendment to the US Constitution in 1951, which limited future presidents to two consecutive four-year terms after FDR's unprecedented twelve-year tenure in office, the expectation of a regular, peaceful rotation of executive power between Republicans and Democrats became entrenched among elites and the voting public alike.[24]

With the resignation of President Richard M. Nixon after the Watergate scandal in 1974, however, a faction of the Republican Party began to believe that there was something terribly unfair about how Nixon had been treated. The aforementioned Roger Stone, for example, was an enthusiastic player in various "dirty tricks" to support Nixon's 1972 presidential campaign. (Stone was just twenty years old at the time.) From Stone's perspective,

Republicans and Democrats alike engaged in such tactics during elections; this was simply the nature of hardball politics. Reflecting on Nixon's resignation, Stone later wrote: "far from being a perpetrator, Nixon was a victim ... of a conspiracy by the judges, lawyers, press and committee that relentlessly persecuted him." Republican election consultant Paul Manafort, with whom Stone later worked, also cut his political teeth in the 1972 Nixon presidential campaign. Pat Buchanan, a special assistant to President Nixon, later gained considerable influence as a proponent of far-right isolationist views within the Republican party – in many ways, a forerunner to Trump himself.[25]

Republican alumni of Nixon's Justice Department were also instrumental in promoting the formal constitutional theory of the "unitary executive," that is, the idea that Article II of the US Constitution confers incredibly broad powers on the president to oversee and control the entire executive branch of government without congressional oversight. They argued that reforms enacted by Congress after Watergate under Presidents Gerald Ford and Jimmy Carter had left the presidency weak and ineffective, and that this must be reversed as quickly as possible to restore America's effectiveness and position in the world. Supporters of this viewpoint were thrilled by President Reagan's Supreme Court nomination of Robert Bork, who, as Nixon's solicitor general, played a central role in the October 1973 firing of Watergate Special Prosecutor Archibald Cox – the "Saturday Night Massacre." When the Democratic Senate majority torpedoed Bork's nomination, Republican anger at the judicial establishment grew, as did the conviction that it was really dominated by liberals working in tandem with the Democratic Party.

By the time of President George W. Bush's election in 2000, advocates of the unitary executive theory – including

Vice President Dick Cheney, himself a veteran of the Nixon White House – had become a dominant influence within the Republican Party establishment. Bush's supporters cited the theory to justify a number of extraordinary presidential decisions after the terrorist attacks of 9/11, including the use of torture to extract information from prisoners of war, the labeling of US citizens as "enemy combatants" deprived of usual legal protections, and the wiretapping of American phones without prior judicial approval.[26]

Some critics argue that President Barack Obama did too little to distance himself from unitary executive theory during his own two terms in office – particularly in the way he conducted American foreign policy – implicating the Democratic Party as well in the uncontrolled expansion of executive power in the US political system. The Biden administration, too, has frequently relied on executive orders to circumvent congressional deadlock. Be that as it may, there can be little doubt that President Trump expanded the theory in ways that neither Obama nor George W. Bush would have even imagined. During a complaint about the Mueller probe of Russian interference in the 2016 presidential elections, Trump stated his views quite explicitly, in his typical tortured syntax: "I have an Article II, where I have the right to do whatever I want as president." Combining this hyperbolic definition of unitary executive theory with Republican rage against "unelected bureaucrats" who were thwarting Trump's agenda, we can understand the emergence of the main political binary embraced by the right in the Trump era: Trump is a decisive president representing the last defense of "real America" against the deep state. Whatever the original intent of the legal academics who have promoted unitary executive theory, it is easy to see how such a dichotomy reinforces other rightwing conspiracy theories

– especially the dangerous QAnon fantasy that former President Trump is actually a hero struggling to defeat a global network of financial elites and pedophiles operating within the US government.[27]

* * *

We are now in a position to see how the conflation of the modern administrative state with a nefarious deep state has become so entrenched in American political discourse – and in the politics of countries far beyond American shores. The combination of a libertarian suspicion of "creeping socialism," Christian nationalist resentment at perceived assaults on religious liberty by the "secular state," and anger at encroachments on Republican presidential power by "liberal judges and bureaucrats" has become a recipe for general fury at the US administrative state in its entirety. The battle against the deep state, for all these diverse factions, has gradually morphed into a struggle of good against evil. Those who still wish to defend an ongoing significant role for the state in providing public goods (schools, roads, airports, and health inspectors, for example) and welfare protection are painted as communist apologists, crusading atheists, and victims of "Trump derangement syndrome" – all at the same time. Not surprisingly, such a poisoned political discourse generates no progress toward consensus, only shouting matches and worse.

What the right today fails to notice, however, is that the seemingly unshakable alignment of libertarianism, Christian nationalism, and executive power advocates against the deep state is only superficial. These three camps may agree on a common enemy, but their visions of the country's future are utterly at odds. Libertarians obviously don't want to live under the strict enforcement of religious morality, particularly when it poses a direct threat to individual liberty. The sacred texts of libertarianism are themselves hardly supportive of Christian values: Ayn Rand was famously atheistic, and Hayek was an avowed agnostic.

Religious nationalists, for their part, might think they prefer vastly expanded power for the executive branch – as long as the occupant of the White House is, like Trump, willing to promote overt Christianity in government. But a powerful executive is not always guaranteed to take the side of religious over secular principles. Nor do the religious principles of various Christian nationalists themselves necessarily coincide. It's not as if the theological differences among Protestants, Catholics, Mormons, and other Christian faith communities have somehow disappeared, let alone the differences between Christians and adherents of other religions. The moment the administrative state is fully dismantled, these religious divisions will immediately come once again to the fore – as indeed they already have in early court cases about the repeal of *Roe v. Wade*.

Nor can supporters of unitary executive theory be said to be in any deep philosophical alignment with libertarianism. One must do serious mental cartwheels to make a defense of absolute control by the president over the vast powers of the executive branch somehow seem consistent with keeping that government to its minimally possible size and scope. Supporters of "originalism" as an approach to constitutional law must now tie themselves into intellectual knots to demonstrate that the founders, having just overthrown the tyranny of King George III, really wanted to vest unbridled political power in a new presidency practically unchecked by the other two branches of government.

Not only is the unholy alliance of libertarians, Christian nationalists, and unitary executive theorists intellectually inconsistent, it opens the door to yet another strain of antiliberal politics – namely, unabashed support for one-man rule, unblocked by any legal or constitutional niceties. Those of us more inclined to support democratic ideals may find it difficult to empathize with such views, but they are not that rare in the larger sweep of human history. Indeed, rule by an autocrat who portrays himself as a kind of "father of the nation" has been a common mode of political organization for millennia. In this respect, the presidency of Donald Trump represented just one instance of a powerful global movement to reestablish personalistic rule as the dominant type of government, as was the case in the premodern era.

As disturbing as democratic backsliding might be, the attack on the modern state poses an even graver challenge. Having demonized civil servants and judiciaries as disloyal and hidden deep states, contemporary anti-state movements have taken aim at some of the core institutions that have shaped the modern world for the better. Dreams of a stateless libertarian society, a "restored" Christian *völkish* community, or a smoothly functioning order run by an all-powerful ruler are unlikely to be workable in today's complex and interdependent world. These political philosophies are all utopian (or dystopian). Instead, the alternative to the modern state and its specialized agencies and expertise is really none of these things but, instead, as we show in the next chapter, the return of a much older form of government: the rule of narcissistic male leaders who treat the state as a family business of sorts, doling out state assets to their relatives and cronies as rewards for their loyalty.

Life under this sort of rule will be very bad news for libertarians, who will quickly discover what a state without regularized administrative procedures, expert-staffed agencies, and an independent judiciary is really like. Liberty and constitutional freedoms will be little more than slogans, and markets will certainly not be free. Personalistic rule will be equally bad news for religious communities who happen to disagree with the particular brand of orthodox belief supported by the rulers – that is, the vast majority of believers in a religiously diverse country like the United States. Even supporters of unitary executive theory will learn just how quickly unchecked presidential power will degenerate into utter lawlessness and weakness once personalistic rule is fully consolidated. Their almighty leader will pull on levers attached to nothing but networks of cronies and loyalists. And from a public policy perspective, the return of premodern forms of rule and the destruction of professional government administration will plunge us back into the poor, unhealthy, and unsafe world that the modern state has helped much of humanity to overcome. But now the threat is not simply to one society or another, but to the entire human species.

For this reason, we cannot fully understand the assault on the state by examining the United States alone. Americans like to think of our country as "exceptional," but the Trump phenomenon is unfortunately anything but that. Trumpism is only part of a much larger global trend toward the replacement of modern civic government with much older personalistic forms of political order. To see this phenomenon more clearly, we need to put the US case into comparative global perspective.

Unfortunately, to date, analysis of the threat to modern governance has also been hampered by the widespread tendency to confuse it with a quite different issue: the future of global democracy. Democracy, to be sure, is under attack around the world. But as we have seen in the United States, even democratically elected leaders can gravely damage the integrity of the civil service and the independence of the judiciary. Free and fair elections by themselves cannot guarantee that those elected to lead

42

their countries will respect the legal rules and professional expertise that are the foundation of effective modern governance.

Before we can successfully pinpoint the primary causes and symptoms of the assault on the state, then, we need to show more clearly why the threat to modern government has been missed by scholars, journalists, and policymakers who have focused solely on the "democracy debate." Having worried so much about the sort of regime change that occurs when authoritarian rulers take power from democratically elected leaders, analysts have failed to notice an even more fundamental form of regime transformation going on around our world – namely, a truly historic shift away from the impersonal rule of law to the personalistic rule of men. We even lack the vocabulary to describe this shift properly. When we see powerful executives attacking the integrity of their own state agencies and judiciaries, we respond by downgrading their countries' democracy rankings – even if these leaders were freely chosen by the majority of voters in relatively fair elections. The next chapter will show how moving beyond the democracy debate can give us the conceptual tools we need to confront the assault on the state more effectively.

3

Beyond the Democracy Debate

In the spring of 2021, India's international reputation took a major hit. Three of the premier organizations that judge the state of freedom and democracy in the world – Freedom House, Varieties of Democracy (V-Dem), and the Economist Intelligence Unit – simultaneously downgraded India's ranking. For decades, India had defied the conventional wisdom of political scientists that only rich countries can become and remain democratic. But in this report, Freedom House reduced India's status from "free" to "partly free." V-Dem's evaluation was even more damning, classifying India as an "electoral autocracy," placing it on the same level as its rival Pakistan and behind Bangladesh. And the *Economist* described India as a "flawed democracy," putting it in 53rd place in the world rankings. Prime Minister Narendra Modi and his ruling party, the BJP, had mostly brushed off these kinds of criticism in previous years (sometimes quietly shuttering foreign organizations such as Amnesty International), but this time the categorical shift and unanimity of judgments across the "Western" world cut to the bone.

Reaction from the Indian government was swift. Its foreign ministry called the Freedom House report "inaccurate and distorted" and objected that India "did not need sermons, especially from those who cannot get their basics right." The defensiveness and sense of insult was palpable. "You use the dichotomy of democracy and autocracy," Foreign Minister Subrahmanyam Jaishankar complained with a slight nod to postcolonial pride; "You want the truthful answer ... it is called hypocrisy. So they invent their rules, their parameters, they pass their judgements and then make out as though this is some kind of global exercise."[1]

India is hardly alone in objecting to its declining ranking in global democracy indexes. In 2020, Freedom House began speaking of Hungary as a "hybrid regime" that had lost its prior status as a semi-consolidated democracy. The Orbán government's wounded response differed little from India's, except for the dash of antisemitism thrown in. Zoltán Kovács, Hungary's secretary of state for international communication and relations, wrote on Twitter that Freedom House "was once known as the bipartisan human rights organization. With their [George] Soros funding they've declined, becoming the fist of the party that is the Soros network. Anyone who doesn't conform to their liberal view, gets downgraded."[2]

Of course, supporters of Prime Ministers Modi and Orbán are quite wrong to complain about the declines in India's and Hungary's rankings in global democracy indexes. Indeed, Modi and Orbán themselves are largely responsible for the increasingly authoritarian nature of their governments. Yet their criticisms nevertheless contain a grain of truth. These democracy rankings *are* global exercises. Each of these organizations analyzes almost every country in the world on an annual basis, and a great deal depends upon where countries end up on their lists.

Billions of dollars in aid, tourism, and foreign investment are affected, directly or indirectly, by perceptions of how democratic or authoritarian a country is. The accuracy and use of these democracy rankings can be questioned not only by those who feel slighted or threatened by them, but also by serious students of politics and history. Are these lists really tapping into everything that matters in politics? In fact, thinking purely in terms of democracy versus authoritarianism may obscure as much as it reveals. Prime Ministers Modi and Orbán are certainly authoritarians rather than committed democrats. But their efforts to transform the very nature of political legitimacy in their countries, like those of similar narcissistic male leaders such as Jair Bolsonaro, Boris Johnson, Benjamin Netanyahu, and Donald Trump, are not fully captured with this binary. We need new terms to understand what is at stake, to grasp what is threatening our world.

* * *

To try to recast the debate about contemporary regime change is not an easy task. Few conceptual frameworks in popular discussion and within the social sciences are as widespread and enduring as the presumed division of political regimes into two basic categories – either "democratic" or "authoritarian." Indeed, for most observers today, the study of "regime change" is essentially synonymous with the study of transitions and alternations between democracy and authoritarianism in different world regions. Nearly all the major quantitative databases that track regime change organize their ratings on linear scales, with pure democracy on one pole and pure authoritarianism on the other. Scholars realize, of course, that this conceptual scheme may require more nuance (and scholars love nuance). They have proposed a huge variety of suggested adjustments to the simple

46

"democratic versus authoritarian" dichotomy. Most modifications, however, involve making finer distinctions within these two categories – democracy and authoritarianism "with adjectives," as two leading political scientists have put it. When formerly democratic countries backslide, they are downgraded to the status of "electoral democracies" or even "electoral autocracies" – yet the underlying assumption that all political regimes can be placed precisely on a continuum between the poles of democracy and authoritarianism remains unquestioned. Today, not only university professors but also journalists, diplomats, and most members of the educated public accept the basic division between democracy and authoritarianism as unproblematic.[3]

Yet before the twentieth century, intellectuals and philosophers would have found it very strange to try to categorize types of political order in such simple terms. Contrary to popular myth, political philosophers in ancient Greece did not uphold democratic rule as either particularly desirable or enduring. It would take another two millennia for political theorists such as Montesquieu and Madison to propose broadly constitutional, representative government as a "universally" superior political form. Even then, as today, we wrestle with "democratic" theory as it was articulated and institutionalized in the American and French Revolutions – that is, as inextricably paired with the hypocritical and brutal exclusion of enslaved people, women, those without property, and the populations of conquered nations.

Only in the modern era – and particularly after the defeat of the Nazi regime in World War II and the unfolding of the Cold War – did the commitments of social scientists unite much more openly on the side of socially inclusive democratic institutions. In the wake of the global destruction wrought by the totalitarian regimes of Hitler,

Stalin, and Mao, hoary defenses of "aristocratic virtue" lost intellectual respectability among educated elites. In the new Western consensus synthesized by some of the greats of mid-century American social science, such as sociologist Talcott Parsons, democracy was portrayed as the inevitable and superior endpoint of human political history. Logically, the persistence of authoritarian rule in any guise now appeared atavistic, resting in incomplete or interrupted social "modernization." And as a corollary, ideologies defending authoritarianism were portrayed as dangerously reactionary.[4]

The resulting schema is one in which all politics involves degrees of rule by "the leader" or "the people" (in Greek, the *demos*). There is nothing wrong per se with this approach to analyzing regimes, but, as with any set of categories, the question is whether they fully capture the reality we seek to explain. To be clear: we are fully in agreement with our colleagues Steven Levitsky and Daniel Ziblatt that the global threat to democracy is sadly all too real. They and others who have written about democratic decline in the twenty-first century have performed a major public service by pointing out that democracies are typically not overthrown in a single revolutionary moment, but instead can die gradually, almost imperceptibly, as the informal practices that underpin stable democratic governance erode and political violence gets normalized.[5]

We wish to draw public attention to a different, interconnected problem: the growing threat not only to democracy, but to modern state administration in general – upon which any workable democratic system of governance in the contemporary world must depend. This is a subject that Americans in particular tend to have a hard time discussing, owing to our strong cultural aversion to centralized government in any form. As the political scientist Samuel Huntington pointed out many decades ago, if you ask most Americans to describe the rules for forming a new government, they immediately respond with a list of *restrictions* on government: constitutional checks and balances, bills of individual rights, and rules for federalism and the decentralization of state power. Yet somehow, modern states have to be able to exercise enough authority to transform majority preferences into effective administrative policies. If not, elected officials must remain impotent to carry out the people's will.

The notion of a great divide between democracy and authoritarianism draws our attention to the question of who rules and the conditions under which leaders ascend to power, but it tells us little about how rule is actually conducted. Is political power exercised impartially according to legal principles, or is it utilized to favor well-connected elites and their supporters? Are public policies implemented with competence and effectiveness, or are government officials mostly corrupt and venal? These questions cannot be answered simply by pointing to the presence or absence of free and fair elections in a country. After all, history provides plenty of examples of relatively effective authoritarian regimes – and an even greater number of corrupt democracies with incompetent governments.

In some ways, labeling leaders such as Modi, Orbán, or Trump as simply "anti-democratic" may even play rhetorically into their hands. They and their followers inevitably reply that not only were these leaders genuinely elected to their positions, but that they also represent their "people" more faithfully than the "global liberal elites" who attempt to impose external political standards on their countries. Moreover, such leaders see the dismantling of the "technocratic" state, and the "neoliberal" global order that reinforces it, as their electoral mandate. For their millions of committed supporters, then, today's elected authoritarian leaders sound completely credible when they accuse the global "experts" of being the real authoritarians, while they represent "democracy" in an even "purer" national form. We may vehemently reject such claims as tendentious and self-serving, yet unless we understand why this form of antiliberal rhetoric continues to appeal to so many marginalized social groups in countries around the world, our efforts to diminish the power and influence of elected authoritarian leaders will be hamstrung.

We therefore need to combine the democracy–authoritarianism distinction with another one that can capture the specific pathology we want to explain: the attack on and deconstruction of modern administrative states. Leaders like Modi, Orbán, and Trump not only want to stay in power indefinitely; they also cement their power by treating state agencies as their personal property and passing out state assets to friends and cronies in return for unquestioning loyalty. Given the contemporary broad-based assault on the state that we examined in the last chapter, such moves can even be portrayed as more "democratic" than efforts to defend the role of administrative expertise in government decision-making.

To understand our contemporary predicament, then, we must introduce a second dimension of regime type, one not reducible to democracy or authoritarianism: namely, personalism versus proceduralism. More than a century ago, the German sociologist Max Weber alerted us to this crucial distinction, which has been obscured in our current debates about the decline of global democracy. Rather than focusing on the selection of leaders, Weber considered the key act of politics to be obedience to the leader's command. After all, without obedience to commands there can be no government, no matter how it is chosen.[6]

Weber argued that the key question of politics is simply this: why do state officials agree to obey the leader's orders? Subordinating one's will entirely to that of another is not something most human beings tend to do on a regular basis. Of course, leaders can obtain temporary obedience instrumentally, by constantly rewarding their staff with special benefits or threatening them with punishment; but if these are the only reasons for official compliance with the leader's orders, state administration will be terribly fragile. As soon as the rewards and punishments are removed, everyone will pursue their own interests again without regard to the leader's preferences, and the "state" will fall apart. For political organization to endure over time, then, those who obey the leader must feel that they have a duty, and not only a self-interest incentive, to do so.

The core link in establishing a state is between the leader and his or her administrative "staff." Weber's key insight was that there are really only two ways that political order can be established in a way that makes it seem "legitimate" to those who implement the leader's decisions: this relationship can be highly personal and intimate, or it can be impersonal and legalistic. Put differently, the staff obeys because of a sense of duty to the person of the leader or because of a sense of duty to the law. For much of human history, the obedience of state officials was based primarily on personal relationships. During periods of social crisis, followers might obey orders under the spell of a leader's personal charisma. But charismatic leadership generally does not last long. To endure over time, the personal bond between leaders and their staff typically requires that both see themselves as defending the sacred traditions of their larger community.

For this reason, one of the most common ways to establish personalist political authority is to pose as the "father" of one's people. The equation of the political leader with the (male) head of the household generates a regime type Weber termed "patrimonialism." Patrimonial regimes in which state officials obey the leader because they truly see him as the "father figure" defending the entire community are actually one of the most common forms of political rule. The patrimonial bond, when durable, is emotional, one of respect, friendship, and devotion, embodied in the beloved monarch whose royal lineage had ruled since "time immemorial." Finding a loyal staff is not easy, so in its purest form "patrimonialism" amounts to rule by the family and friends of the leader. The patrimonial ruler and his staff fuse administration with personal authority, considering the state itself to be a "family business" of sorts. And gender matters here too: the image of the ruler as the benevolent "father" tends to reinforce broader stereotypes of men as powerful and active, and women as subordinate and passive. For this reason, patrimonial leaders almost always denounce movements to defend the rights of women and sexual minorities as an existential threat.[7]

Patrimonial rule characterized much of the premodern world. In most times and places, the state as we now understand it, as a set of impersonal institutions, regulations, and bureaucracies separate from the person and personality of the ruler, simply did not exist. Understanding the nature and prevalence of patrimonial rule is crucial to appreciating what threatens the West today. We can illustrate the main features of patrimonial rule through some telling examples in Eurasia, Africa, Latin America, and Asia: Russia under the Romanovs, Ethiopia under Emperor Haile Selassie, the Dominican Republic under Rafael Trujillo, and the Philippines under President Ferdinand Marcos. As we will see, despite their differences, these cases all show quite clearly what happens to the state when the person of the leader himself becomes the dominant ruling principle.

* * *

In his influential treatment of Russian history, Harvard historian Richard Pipes argued that whereas in England, France, and Spain the modern Western state began to take shape as an "entity separate from the ruler" as far back as the twelfth and thirteenth centuries, in Russia the core of political authority remained "the private domain of the prince or tsar." The basis of obedience was not to the office or the law but to the person. Pipes explicitly invokes the term "patrimonialism" to describe Russia under the old regime: "There is considerable advantage in retaining the term 'patrimonial' to define a regime where the rights of sovereignty and those of ownership blend to the point of becoming indistinguishable, and political power is exercised in same manner as economic power." In Russia, the essence of the old regime was the absence of any distinction between sovereignty and ownership – the "state" was the family business of the tsars – and this, more than anything, encapsulates the idea of patrimonialism.[8]

The impressive external power of the tsarist order masked systemic internal weaknesses. Patrimonial rule in Russia was never efficient, nor was it especially despotic. The tsars' lofty claims of absolute power over "all the Russias" did not accurately mirror the reality of a weak "state" consisting of personal retainers and local nobles – each with his own "patrimonial" power – spread out over a vast territory. At the beginning of the nineteenth century, Russian rulers did not have access to the most rudimentary knowledge of their own empire: even the names of many of its settlements were unknown, not subject to a comprehensive census that only a modern bureaucratic state could execute. Later in the same century, in the face of a devastating famine, the state lacked the knowledge and capacity on the ground to supply relief in many areas.[9]

Critics of this image of the Russian Empire as patrimonial maintain that it reflects an anti-Russian bias. They argue that not only did key Russian rulers such as Peter the Great and Catherine the Great lay the groundwork for many elements of modern state administration, but the path of state development in the West was not all that different. To a certain extent, both points are true. Russia does have a "legal" strand in its state history, and, by the nineteenth century, the monarchy had made considerable (if somewhat halting) efforts to create modern judiciaries and bureaucracies. Political rule in the West also has a patrimonial background. In the Netherlands during the sixteenth and seventeenth centuries, as Julia Adams has shown, powerful patrician men dominated politics and viewed their rule as an extension of their economic interests. And it was King Louis XIV's reign in seventeenth-century France that inspired the quintessential statement of patrimonial prerogative: *"L'état, c'est moi."*[10]

There were, then, similarities in political developments between Russia and the West – but the divergences are simply too stark to ignore. By the beginning of the twentieth century, the rule of powerful families and monarchs of the Netherlands, England, and France was ultimately subordinated to impersonal states bound to constitutions (whether written or unwritten) and the rule of law. In Russia, tsars resisted this until the very end, and the ideal of patrimonialism remained powerful. Staffing of ministries and bureaucracies remained arbitrary and dependent on personal access, and advisors constantly competed for the tsar's personal attention. Commoners addressed the tsar in writing on matters great and trivial in the hopes of circumventing the inefficiency and disinterest of the Russian state bureaucracy. On the eve of the Russian Revolution of

1917, Russia's last tsar, Nicholas II, was still referred to by his closest advisors as *batushka* (little father).

Yet patrimonial rule is hardly unique to historical Russia. It has also been especially pronounced in the developing world. The Ethiopian "state" under Emperor Hailie Selassie from 1930 to 1974, for example, amounted to little more than an extension of his court and his personality. Appointing incompetent ministers ensured that they would not outshine the Emperor and would be personally dependent, competing among themselves for the attentions of the exalted one. According to an informant cited in Ryszard Kapuściński's colorful account: "Not only did the Emperor decide on all promotions, but he also communicated each one personally. He alone. He filled the posts at the summit of the hierarchy, and also its lower and middle levels. He appointed postmasters, headmasters of schools, police constables, all of the most ordinary office employees, estate managers, brewery directors, managers of hospitals and hotels – and let me say it again, he chose them personally." The Emperor oversaw even the most trivial assignments because the source of power was not "the state or any institution," but the person of the Emperor himself.[11]

Hailie Selassie was an extreme case. How many leaders have retainers whose sole job is to place cushions under the emperor's feet while he is sitting on his throne so that they do not dangle in the air? But less pronounced, if no less dysfunctional, versions of such subservience to the "father of the nation" are to be found throughout the world, and they illustrate different facets of patrimonial rule. Take for example the issue of control over economic assets. Those of us living in the West typically assume that political power follows from great wealth, but under patrimonial rule the reverse is true: great wealth flows from political power. Rafael Trujillo, ruler of the Dominican Republic from 1930 to 1961, built the state not so much to regulate and protect society but rather to extend his personal rule and extract resources from society. Like Selassie, he exhibited megalomaniacal tendencies. In his first term in office, Pico Duarte, the highest mountain in the Antilles, received a new name: Pico Trujillo. Santo Domingo, the capital city, was renamed Ciudad Trujillo. Generalissimo Trujillo appointed his son, Ramfis, as a full colonel in the army at the age of four, a brigadier general at the age of fourteen, and chief of staff of the air force at age twenty-three. At the time of his overthrow in 1961, Trujillo had more statues of himself spread throughout the country than any other world leader.

Beyond these somewhat comical indicators more or less typical of strongmen everywhere, perhaps of greater importance is the fate of the Dominican state itself. In 1934, Trujillo imposed a series of state monopolies on salt, meat, and rice that made him the country's richest man, and he used his power to expand his economic holdings over the next two decades. He forced owners of industrial enterprises to sell their shares and took a cut of the funding for public works contracts. Following World War II, Trujillo expanded his holdings into cement, chocolate, cardboard, flour, paint, liquor, and, most crucially, sugar. By 1956, three-quarters of all sugar mills in the country were in his hands. Trujillo's state amounted to little more than a vehicle for transferring wealth from society to himself, his family, and a small and rotating coterie of distributional beneficiaries. To the extent an official ideology existed, it was purely patrimonial: Trujillo portrayed himself as the father of the Dominican nation and the builder of its state, even if this state was inseparable from the interests of Trujillo himself.[12]

Patrimonial rule can also be found in postcolonial Asia. A good example is the Philippines under Ferdinand

Marcos, who ruled from 1965 to 1986. After winning the presidency in 1965, Marcos engineered the declaration of martial law in 1972. Although even before Marcos's rule, Philippine party politics revolved around patronage, the country's state institutions had retained a measure of autonomy from powerholders. This changed quite dramatically after 1972, providing a stark example of a general trend under patrimonial regimes: the dismantling and harvesting of a nascent state bureaucracy for personal ends.

Like other patrimonial rulers, Marcos depicted himself as the "father" of his nation, promoting the myth of his "heroism and courage" as an anti-Japanese guerrilla during World War II. Such tales of bravery under fire were mostly fabrications. In fact, during the occupation Marcos operated a private extortion and theft racket in his home region of Illocos Norte. Once in power, he began to fuse independent state institutions with his household, staffing them primarily with friends and family. His personal driver, Fabian Ver, the relative of a close friend, became Marcos's head of security and later chief of the secret police. Ver, along with his three sons, directed both the Presidential Security Command and the National Intelligence Coordinating Agency.

Marcos also captured the judiciary, undermining its independence, primarily through his power to dismiss any judge arbitrarily. Family members ruled over much of the state apparatus and turned it into a family business. His wife Imelda Marcos's positions included governor of Metro Manila, ambassador at large, and minister of human settlements – the latter a bureaucracy created from scratch for her own aggrandizement. Imelda's brother, Benjamin "Kokoy" Romualdez, ran the Bureau of Customs, the General Auditing Commission, and the Bureau of Internal Revenue. Her sister, Alita Martel, held the "franchise" of the Central Bank and the Department of Agriculture. The president's brother, Pacifico Marcos, headed the Medicare Commission. And his mother directed the Rice and Corn Administration. Marcos's sister was governor of his home province until his son, Ferdinand Jr. – who in 2022 became president of the Philippines – took over the post.[13]

These examples of patrimonial rule may seem either shocking or tawdry, but they are in no way unusual. In fact, patrimonial forms of rule have characterized politics throughout most of human history. At their best, patrimonial states do provide a modicum of order, and when combined with at least moderately functional legal institutions, they can provide their subjects with a better life than might be had under conditions of pure anarchy or the decentralized rule of competing feudal lords. If the alternative is political chaos and violence, patrimonial order may well appear preferable to many people.

But daily life under patrimonialism is never fully predictable, as the arbitrary whims of the ruler and his personal coterie continually interfere with the regular functioning of state agencies. Thus, despite its relatively well-developed legal system, the tsarist state in Russia could do little to prevent anti-Jewish pogroms throughout the last quarter of the nineteenth and first decade of the twentieth century, and it collapsed entirely after repeated defeats to the German military during World War I. Haile Selassie's regime was overthrown by a Marxist-Leninist coup in 1974; repeating the fate of Tsar Nicholas II, Selassie was later murdered by Ethiopia's new revolutionary leaders. Rafael Trujillo's patrimonial regime tortured and killed thousands of innocent civilians during his decades of rule until his assassination in 1961. And Ferdinand Marcos's regime, seemingly secure in its dictatorial power, was swept away suddenly in the People Power Revolution of 1986. Patrimonial rule appears to be stable and powerful, yet at its core, it is brutal, inefficient, and susceptible to unexpected collapse.

Nor do patrimonial regimes create a favorable environment for sustainable economic growth and development. At best they supply poorly functioning institutions, and at worst they actively prey on the economy. And where they fail spectacularly is in responding to complex crises of natural disasters, war, and epidemics. The history of much of the world is that of famines, military catastrophe, and plagues, and many of these tragedies are a direct result of the subordination of the state to the rule of men.

* * *

Given the patterns of previous human history, it is all the more remarkable that the domination of the patrimonial principle gave way to legal forms of impersonal governance in most of the modern West by the twentieth century. This happened in fits and starts, with plenty of setbacks and reversals along the way. But ultimately, the advent of modern capitalism and modern military organization transformed politics in Europe and North America by generating modern bureaucracies, staffed by a civil service of educated professionals, who followed legal rules and procedures and who were recruited on the basis of merit rather than personal relationships. The primary grounds on which commands were obeyed shifted from duty to the person of the ruler to duty to the impersonal requirements of the rules themselves. When state bureaucracies worked well, they made the modern world powerful, productive, and relatively safe. The end point of modern state-building is the creation of a civil service recruited on the basis of merit, promoted on the basis of expertise, and protected from political depredation by consistently enforced laws.

Why are impersonal bureaucracies so important? Why did the development of modern warfare and capitalism require their creation? Simply put, modern states provide goods and services that markets do not provide on their own but need in order to function well. As mainstream economics has established, self-interested individuals on their own typically won't volunteer to help produce public goods – that is, goods that benefit all of us collectively, but which we can each enjoy even if we did not personally contribute to them. Take, for example, clean air. Having fresh air to breathe is obviously vastly preferable to choking on thick smog, but this fact on its own isn't going to stop self-interested people from driving their cars. If I abstain from driving while everybody else around me continues to do so, I'm just a sucker: it now takes me much longer to get from place to place, and I still have to breathe the same polluted air as everyone else. Hence, as the economist Mancur Olson showed long ago, there has to be some other incentive at work for most people to contribute to public goods. Typically, then, large-scale public goods provision comes not from the market, but from the state.[14]

Many libertarians seem to have forgotten this essential point. Public goods such as subsidized systems of transportation, public schools, municipal police forces, impartial courts, national defense, and public health and safety are not goods that markets provide on their own – yet modern market economies need all of them in order to function. Patrimonial regimes may sometimes provide these as well, but only as an extension of the interests of the ruler's household. Because patrimonial rules run the state as a "family business," each of these public goods can be commandeered for the private benefit of the ruler and his cronies at any time – rendering them unpredictable and inefficient. Public roads may be shut down for the private use of the president's motorcade. Public schools may be forced to devote more and more class time to myths about the greatness of the leader. Police forces, courts, and armies may be required to obey the dictates of the "father of the nation" at the expense of fairness and competence. And in the end, both national defense and public health will likely be sacrificed in favor of the patrimonial ruler's personal whims.

This is why, over time, countries with modern legal states have so dramatically outperformed their patrimonial competitors. Indeed, the "rise of the West" over the past five centuries to a position of unparalleled global power and wealth would be unthinkable without the evolution of modern state agencies and legal systems. To be sure, European and North American imperialism and slavery also played highly significant roles in the establishment of Western hegemony over much of Asia, Africa, and Latin America. Western colonial rule over conquered peoples was itself often carried out through the arbitrary patrimonial power of colonial administrators, showing the deep hypocrisy of Western claims to be more "civilized" than those they subordinated. Yet the brutality of Western imperialism by itself does not explain why a few relatively tiny and historically backward countries of Northern Europe – such as Britain, Belgium, and the Netherlands, British settler colonial societies such as the United States, Canada, and Australia, and a few older European states like France, Spain, and Portugal – were able to subjugate the vast majority of the planet by the end of the nineteenth century. What all these regimes had in common was the development, to a greater or lesser extent, of modern state institutions that had replaced or modified the patrimonial politics of Europe during the Middle Ages.

It is important to separate the process of modern state-building from democracy. The two do not always coincide. Historically, impersonal bureaucracies staffed by experts and operating according to the rule of law could and frequently did evolve in nondemocratic contexts. Germany in the half century before World War I stands out as the best example of this. Government remained nonparliamentary (ministers were appointed by the Kaiser), but it possessed an efficient bureaucracy staffed by personnel with a sense of duty to the state rather than any leader. In the post-World War II era, Singapore stands out as an authoritarian but nonpatrimonial state; it has long been known for its relatively uncorrupt bureaucracy and efficient provision of public goods. Even communist states such as the Soviet Union and post-Mao China at various points of time have been able to construct reasonable facsimiles of modern administrative apparatuses that provide impressive public goods such as schools, roads, and public health systems. None of these examples necessarily deserves praise or admiration, but they do demonstrate the need to think of democratization and the evolution of the modern state along different axes.

Of course, over the course of human history, patrimonial and bureaucratic modes of administration have often coexisted. One can readily identify elements of "bureaucracy" in ancient Egypt and "patrimonialism" in twentieth-century urban America. But until fairly recently, the process of bureaucratic rationalization, once underway, has tended to be sticky. State bureaucracies have gotten bigger, more complex, and more influential over time. Most scholars have therefore assumed that, with the rise of complex modern administrative states, patrimonial forms of rule would decline in most of the world, save perhaps in economically underdeveloped countries where traditional norms of politics still prevail. Weber himself warned during his lifetime of the reappearance of traditional imperialism under the right conditions, in particular in the anti-capitalist dictatorship emerging in Soviet Russia after 1917. But neither Weber nor later mainstream social scientists anticipated the vengeance with which the patrimonial principle might eventually reassert itself as a competing form of political legitimacy in advanced capitalist societies.[15]

Once we consider this possibility, however, the dichotomy between democracy and authoritarianism seems inadequate to understand the central challenges facing the contemporary world. We therefore need a different typology of regime types. Authoritarian leaders may govern through remarkably effective state bureaucracies. And a leader may be democratically elected but still seek to legitimate his or her rule patrimonially. Increasingly, elected leaders have sought to demolish bureaucratic administrative states built up over decades – the so-called deep state bogeyman we examined in the previous chapter – in favor of rule by family and friends. The consequences of this shift in state legitimacy for the citizenry are profound.

Patrimonialism was the default form of rule in the premodern world. The state was little more than the extended "household" of the ruler; it did not exist as a separate entity. In the developing world, as our examples from Ethiopia, the Dominican Republic, and the Philippines show, the trappings of the modern state – judiciaries, ministries, the police, and various government services – all have "external" form. Ministries are built, civil services exist on paper, and lawyers are trained, but their training, staffing, and operations are subordinated to the interests of the ruling family or clique.

In explaining this phenomenon, scholars have attributed it to the lack of "modernization" in much of the world and have labeled the phenomenon as *neo*-patrimonial to highlight the disparity between modern forms and personalistic reality. But the return of patrimonialism in the major powers of the West itself cannot possibly be chalked up to economic backwardness, weak "modernization," or the cutting-and-pasting of institutional forms to an inappropriate context: not only is the West wealthy, but modern bureaucracies are also Western inventions. Establishing patrimonialism in Western countries such as the United States requires not so much corrupting institutions as deconstructing them.

It is worth pondering for a moment what an extraordinary departure the contemporary assault on the modern state truly is. The return of premodern forms of rule into the modern world contradicts almost everything we thought to be true about the trajectory of political change. Common wisdom simply assumed that once "feudalism" and "imperialism" gave way to democratic nation-states, political history would continue to march forward – not reverse itself. For this reason, the global patrimonial wave of the past two decades or so has gone practically unnoticed. When we focus our attention on the decline of democracy and the rise of "authoritarian populism," it's easy to miss seeing that the modern state as we have known it is also under severe assault.

So how did we get to this point? Having identified the core features of patrimonialism, we now need to explain the remarkable and unexpected political appeal of this form of rule in the twenty-first century. We therefore turn our attention to the initial reemergence of this idea in post-Soviet Russia under President Vladimir Putin, who has served as a model for would-be patrimonial rulers ever since.

4

How Vladimir Putin Resurrected Tsarism

The assault on the modern state began in a country that many had written off as irrelevant to global affairs: post-Soviet Russia. Before the start of the twenty-first century, anti-state social movements on both the right and the left were marginal forces in the developed nations. "Populist" parties arose from time to time in various countries, even gaining seats and ministries in several Western parliaments, but they could offer no credible alternative vision of the political order. Now such an alternative is clear to everyone. Russian President Vladimir Putin's rise to power in the late 1990s, and his reassertion of Russia's great power status over the course of his reign, showed the world that a traditional, personalistic, and imperial regime could still generate significant economic, military, and geopolitical power in the modern era. Putin's personalistic autocracy has thus provided a road map for the consolidation of the "rule of men," and the destruction of the rule of law, for his acolytes and admirers on every continent. With Russia's unprovoked and brutal military invasion of Ukraine, Putin's dark vision of the future has become a direct threat to the entire global order. Even if Putin himself disappears from the scene, understanding just how he was able to rise to his position of near-absolute power in Russia is vital if we want to reverse the patrimonial wave before it is too late.

Writing about this subject is difficult, however. Aren't we just perpetuating what Donald Trump called "the Russia Hoax"? Trump's vituperative attacks on anyone who dares to link Russian politics to events in the United States have been undeniably effective in muddying the waters. Thanks to Trump's tirades, tweets, and "truths," viewers of Fox News and consumers of conservative social media often wrongly assume that the Mueller Report found no evidence of Russian interference with the 2016 presidential election – and that, if anything, the Clinton and Biden families were the ones somehow entangled in murky dealings with sinister post-Soviet figures. As we explore the subject of Putin's global influence, we can already hear the refrain: it's always "Russia, Russia, Russia"!

Such obfuscations and conspiracy theories, like all enduring social myths, contain a grain of truth. Donald Trump really did win the 2016 presidential election under the constitutional rules accepted by all mainstream American politicians, just as surely as Joe Biden defeated Trump in 2020. Nor do we have any factual evidence of the more lurid claims about compromising material Putin might have on the former US President. And while Putin's propaganda machine, powered by Russian-affiliated social media trolls and bots, intervened frequently to undercut Hillary Clinton's candidacy, the best evidence suggests that these interventions did not determine the final election result. Americans really did choose Trump as their president in a free and fair election, and they were not following the will of a foreign dictator in the secrecy of the ballot box. Those who imply that Putin somehow installed Trump in power are drastically overstating their case.

Nor did Putin somehow manipulate Trump once in office like a puppeteer pulling his strings. It is true that Trump did show a strange obsequiousness to Putin. Inviting Russian Foreign Minister Sergei Lavrov and Russian Ambassador to the US Sergei Kislyak to the White House in May 2017, then sharing highly classified information with them, was careless at best. We still don't know precisely what Trump and Putin talked about for more than two hours, with only their interpreters present, at the Helsinki Summit in July 2018. Trump's public disparaging of his own intelligence services at the post-summit press conference remains one of the stranger episodes of his frequently bizarre presidential term. Yet these decisions were all within the very extensive legal parameters given to American presidents in the making of foreign policy. And some of the Trump administration's moves, such as the provision of lethal weaponry to Ukraine, clearly went against Putin's interests – even if Trump himself had to be prodded repeatedly to make such decisions by his advisors in the national security establishment, and even if he tried to trade such military aid for "dirt" on his political opponents. The fact remains that the Mueller Report found no "smoking gun" tying Putin's Kremlin to Trump directly.[1]

Putin, Trump, and other contemporary strongmen don't collaborate through some sort of shadowy conspiratorial cabal. The connections among them are both more direct and in a way more unsettling. Simply put, Putin's model of state-building in Russia has turned out to be genuinely appealing to politicians and to mass publics around the world. As we will see, the reasons Putin's patrimonial form of rule appeals to people on every continent are not so different from those that prompted the majority of Russians to support Putin in the first place. Misleading stereotypes about Russia's "inherent" cultural authoritarianism – the notion that Russians somehow collectively crave a "strong hand" to rule over them – won't get us very far in understanding why Putinism has also found so many admirers in countries as diverse as Hungary, Israel, Brazil, and the United States. Nor can responsibility for Putin's policies be attributed solely to Western foreign policy mistakes. Those who wish to blame NATO expansion for the rise of Putinism will struggle to make sense of how patrimonialism has also emerged within NATO member states like Hungary and Turkey.

To understand the origins of the threat to the modern state we now face, we must reexamine the history of the collapse of the Union of Soviet Socialist Republics and the troubled early years of the post-Soviet Russian Federation. Three factors in particular explain Putin's rise to power: the social dislocation generated by the implosion of the Soviet industrial economy, the arrogance of Western technocratic advisors during Russia's first chaotic post-Soviet decade, and Putin's fortunate timing in building a patrimonial petrostate just at the moment when energy prices rose to an all-time peak. We will deal with each of these factors in turn.

The USSR was a tyrannical one-party regime that surveilled and regulated even the smallest details of social life throughout its vast territory. Its collapse was a triumph for human freedom, allowing oppressed nations in East Europe and Eurasia the opportunity to escape the grip of Soviet imperial domination and releasing the creative energies of highly educated populations throughout the Soviet bloc. No one should mourn its passing.

Yet we won't fully understand the appeal of Vladimir Putin to so many ordinary Russians if we fail to grapple with another side of the Soviet regime. The USSR was not just a run-of-the-mill dictatorship. It was also, as historian Stephen Kotkin has put it, an alternative civilization. Over the course of its seventy-four years of existence, the

Soviet Union created the world's second most powerful military, oversaw the creation of a massive new industrial base, supported cutting-edge scientific breakthroughs in theoretical physics and space exploration, and successfully inculcated a true sense of national pride in Soviet achievements. Ordinary Russians, who were widely understood to be the "leading" nation of the USSR, felt this pride in extra measure. Americans who traveled to what was then the "Russian Soviet Federative Socialist Republic" (or RSFSR) during the Cold War – including the authors – can still recall drinking vodka with Russian hosts who would cheerfully declare that the United States and the Soviet Union had a lot in common: *"My sverkhderzhavy!"* We are the superpowers![2]

Even for the generation of Russians who grew up in the waning years of Soviet power, under Leonid Brezhnev and his septuagenarian successors in the leadership of the Communist Party of the Soviet Union (CPSU), it was hard to imagine any concrete alternative to Soviet life. The vast majority of Soviet citizens in the 1980s had never known anything else, and with international travel severely restricted, few of them had an opportunity to compare their situation with other global models. It is true that Western Sovietologists mostly failed to predict the collapse of the Soviet Union – but so did most people within the USSR, until very late in the process. When Mikhail Gorbachev became General Secretary of the CPSU in March 1985, Western intelligence officials and jaded Soviet intellectuals alike were highly skeptical that the system could ever fundamentally change. The idea that Gorbachev's reform program would lead within seven years to the disintegration of the Soviet bloc, then the Soviet economy, and finally the USSR itself was utterly unthinkable.[3]

Gorbachev came to power with the naive idea that the fundamental problem with the Soviet system was its overreliance on top–down control by party and state bureaucrats. His policy of *perestroika*, or restructuring, was designed to change that as quickly as possible. Letting Soviet citizens speak more openly and participate more fully in decision-making, Gorbachev thought, would unleash a massive outpouring of renewed enthusiasm among Soviet workers and peasants alike, sparking renewed economic growth. The world would then see the "inherent" superiority of socialism, leading to a true renaissance of Soviet power at home and abroad. And during his first three years in power, Gorbachev's plans seemed to be working, as Soviet citizens rejoiced in their newfound freedom of expression and a wave of "Gorbymania" spread throughout the West.[4]

As Gorbachev soon learned, however, the rot within Soviet institutions was far deeper than he had imagined. Once it became clear that Gorbachev was serious about giving local leaders the freedom to make important decisions independent from the CPSU, officials and ordinary citizens throughout the Soviet bloc naturally began to test the boundaries of the possible. Yet Gorbachev was deeply reluctant to restore central control, fearing a return to the old Brezhnev-era forms of bureaucratic "stagnation" he wanted so badly to disrupt.

In June 1989, the independent Polish trade union Solidarity won every contested seat but one in Poland's first truly democratic elections in decades, and Gorbachev did not intervene. In November, the East German regime gave in to demands to dismantle the Berlin Wall, and – to the horror of a young KGB colonel then stationed in Dresden, Vladimir Putin – Gorbachev again did nothing. By the end of the year, the "captive nations" of East-Central Europe had all abandoned the Soviet Bloc to "return to Europe," and still Gorbachev did not protest. Not surprisingly, the non-Russian republics of the Soviet Union, chafing against decades of imperial control from Moscow, soon mounted their own drives for full independence. Even Russia itself, under its first president, Boris Yeltsin, began to push for greater autonomy from the Soviet Union. This time, Gorbachev's ruling elite did resort to military force. The Soviet security services killed hundreds of civilian demonstrators in the Baltic States and Azerbaijan – but fortunately, these efforts were not sustained at the scale that would have reversed the tide of disintegration. By the time a cabal of hardliners from the Soviet military and security services tried to overthrow Gorbachev in a palace coup in August 1991, it was far too late to reassemble the wreckage of Soviet power.[5]

For those living in the non-Russian former Soviet republics, the collapse of the USSR meant a chance to rejoin the world community on a dignified basis. The Baltic States of Estonia, Latvia, and Lithuania could now entertain realistic prospects of joining the European Union and NATO, while other European former Soviet Republics could reorient their foreign policy strategies to embrace European values and institutions, albeit with varying degrees of success. The five new Central Asian states were quickly admitted to the United Nations, their populations freed from imperial control for the first time in centuries. For Russians, however, the final disintegration of Soviet rule meant the end of an empire that could trace its roots back to the seventeenth century. To be sure, the new post-Soviet Russian Federation, even within its internationally recognized boundaries, is still by far the largest country in the world – but as the traumas of post-imperial nations ranging from Germany after World War I to England after World War II illustrate, letting go of empire is never easy.

Worse yet, the end of the USSR inevitably brought with it tremendous economic suffering. The industrialization of the Soviet Union carried out by Joseph Stalin, along with its genocidal violence and reliance on prison camp labor, had created a vast and impressive infrastructure oriented above all toward military production. Soviet steel and cement factories utilized the best technologies available in the 1930s, and the Soviet industrialization effort undeniably contributed to the defeat of Nazi Germany in World War II. By the 1970s, however, this mighty industrial base began slowly to decay. The Soviet agricultural sector, decimated by the horrors of Stalin's drive to force farmers onto party-supervised collective farms, stagnated as well. And without market-based incentives for private investment in newly emerging economic sectors such as consumer goods and information technology, the Soviet planned economy proved exceedingly difficult to reform.

The failure of Gorbachev's *perestroika* and the Soviet implosion of 1991 thus also inevitably meant the irrevocable destruction of the top–down coordinating mechanisms of the Soviet economy. Contrary to the rosy forecasts of many Western economists, however, the end of the planning system did not mean a quick "transition to the market." Neither Soviet industrial enterprises nor Soviet farms were designed to compete for profits in a full-fledged market economy. From a Western capitalist perspective, the vast majority of these enterprises outside the energy and minerals sectors were hopelessly uncompetitive. Viewed in the cold light of market rationality, they were not "assets" to be redistributed. They were distressed debt that had previously been propped up by state subsidies, paid for by profits from Soviet oil and gas exports, arms sales, and the state alcohol monopoly.

Imagine, then, what it felt like as a Russian worker in a large industrial plant somewhere in Central Russia to go, seemingly overnight, from being lauded in Communist Party propaganda as a "heroic proletarian" defending Soviet power to being seen as part of a "superfluous" workforce requiring immediate downsizing. Threats of unemployment in outmoded economic sectors are never easy to accept, as coalminers in northern England and steelworkers in Gary, Indiana would surely agree. Add to this the formerly exalted official status of blue-collar labor in a "workers' state," and the anger and confusion of millions of Russian urban and rural workers after 1991 is even more understandable.[6]

For most of the Russian population, then, the Soviet collapse was thus a triple whammy. The loss of super-power status, the loss of economic livelihood, and the loss of a meaningful place in the new social order all transpired simultaneously. Once early dreams of a quick return to economic prosperity and integration with the West were dashed, tens of millions of Russian workers, farmers, and officials became increasingly disillusioned and alienated. In such an environment, it is hardly surprising that conspiracy theories about "who was to blame" began to spread rapidly. The truth – that Gorbachev was a misguided Leninist idealist who genuinely believed that the Soviet system would thrive in the absence of centralized party control, but who had turned out to be dead wrong about that, accidentally destroying the Soviet Union itself – strained credulity. It was much easier to believe that some dark forces in the West had conspired with various Russian traitors to turn Gorbachev against his own people and to destroy the only competitor to the American global liberal order. To this day, Russians tend to believe in anti-Western conspiracy theories of this sort. There is growing evidence that Putin believed in them himself.[7]

Gorbachev's resignation as President of the Soviet Union and the formal breakup of the USSR in December 1991 marked what social scientists call a "critical juncture" in history – a time when massive uncertainty about the future and the disruption of old institutions can open up new possibilities for human action. The atmosphere in 1992 within the newly independent Russian Federation, now led by the democratically elected President Boris Yeltsin, was one of great anxiety, but also of genuine hope. Although such optimism was not destined to last long, pro-Western and pro-American sentiment within Russian society was then quite widespread, as the authors can personally attest from their travels in Russia at the time. Countless Russian citizens looked forward to what they hoped would be a full-fledged integration with Europe, once the initial pain of "transition" was over. President Yeltsin himself pledged that his economic reforms would produce "concrete results" within a year, further raising popular expectations.[8]

At the same time, any dispassionate observer could see that the severity of the post-Soviet economic crisis, along with simmering social resentment among those who had benefited from the old system, might soon undercut Yeltsin's rosy promises of a better future. To seize this once-in-a-generation opportunity to remake the world order, while avoiding the worst-case scenario of a return to Russian authoritarianism and imperialism, would require a unified, far-sighted, and carefully crafted Western response. Unfortunately, no such response was forthcoming.

Let us be clear: the West is not to blame for Russia's failure to consolidate democracy in the years after 1991. President Yeltsin and his advisors made their own decisions about how to proceed with political and economic reform. It was Yeltsin who decided to use violent force to disband the first post-Soviet Russian parliament in 1993. It was Yeltsin who ordered the bloody military invasion of Chechnya in 1994. And it was Yeltsin who, in the end, decided to appoint the head of the security services, former KGB Colonel Vladimir Putin, as his chosen successor in 1999. Ever since, Putin has called the shots in the Kremlin, with any residual Western influence fading very quickly. Finally, it is Putin and his minions who must bear full responsibility for the bloody, illegal invasion of Ukraine – not the West.

Still, while it's a mistake to hold the West somehow solely responsible for Russia's depressing post-Soviet evolution, Western advice to Yeltsin's government after the Soviet collapse clearly didn't help ensure the consolidation of Russian democracy, either. In hindsight, Western policy to assist with the formidable challenges facing Russia after the end of communism should have emphasized three things above all. First, the West should have understood that, for democratic consolidation to be possible, the Russian state institutions inherited from the Soviet Leninist regime first needed to be reformed on the basis of the rule of law. Second, Western policymakers needed to be honest with their Russian partners: the economic pain of dealing with the Soviet legacy was bound to last for a generation, and great humility about the short-term effects of policy interventions was therefore in order. Finally, Western leaders and advisors needed to recognize that the turning point of 1991 might be the only opportunity in at least a generation to try to rebuild Russian state power on the basis of the rule of law, and that helping to support this effort should be the highest possible foreign policy priority. Even if the West had gotten all of these things right, post-Soviet Russian reform efforts might still have failed – but the odds of success would have been at least a bit higher.

Sadly, Western policy during the 1990s was built on precisely the opposite assumptions. Instead of focusing together with Western-oriented Russian elites on the recon-struction of Russian state institutions, Western advisors assumed that the first task should be to create a "market economy" as fast as possible. Instead of being humble in the face of the daunting social challenges ahead, Western advisors trumpeted the superiority of their policy recommendations in a way that came across to most Russians as arrogant and unfeeling. And instead of prioritizing the rebuilding of Russia as a long-term investment in a peaceful global order, the West celebrated the "end of history," enjoyed the economic boost of the "peace dividend," and soon began ignoring Russia altogether.[9]

Behind all of these critical errors was a tragic historic coincidence: the collapse of the Soviet Union transpired during the heyday of an economic doctrine appropriately labeled "the Washington Consensus" – that is, the idea that a simple formula for capitalist reforms, if adopted by a determined elite, would always generate economic efficiency and growth in any country where it was tried. The breakup of the Soviet planned economy appeared to validate this market fundamentalism: if the most successful state-run economic system in history had collapsed so miserably, surely this proved that the state should simply get out of economic decision making everywhere and let the market work its magic. Thus, almost no attention was paid to reforming post-Soviet state institutions themselves. Yet this was desperately needed.

Russia's state bureaucracy, after all, had not been designed to preside over a democratic capitalist economy and society. It thus lacked many of the most basic capacities we take for granted in the West. The post-Soviet Russian legal system was capable of resolving criminal, civil, and economic disputes at the local level with some efficacy, but it suffered from the after-effects of decades of political interference by high-ranking communist officials in cases that threatened the party-state. It was hardly prepared to play the role of a full-fledged independent judiciary and enforcer of private property rights in a democratic market society. The post-Soviet Russian system for financial regulation, set up initially to promote the "fulfillment and overfulfillment" of central plan targets, had not developed any legal mechanisms for managing a convertible currency, for prosecuting white-collar crime in a fair and transparent manner, or for regulating private investment. There were also huge gaps in the formal legislation necessary for managing a modern market economy. To take one remarkable example, the Russian Federation had no comprehensive legal code allowing for the private ownership of land until the early Putin era. Finally, while competent professionals trained in the Soviet era continued to work diligently for low wages in the post-Soviet Russian state bureaucracy – many of them women with decades of experience in their areas of expertise – there was no organized public campaign to recruit idealistic young Russians to commit themselves anew to public state service.[10]

But Western advisors celebrating the collapse of the Soviet state were in no mood to discuss the re-creation of a new one. As the nations of East-Central Europe began to break away from the Soviet bloc in 1989, experts from the International Monetary Fund, the World Bank, and the Organization for Economic Cooperation and Development all repeated the same mantra: post-communist reformers should work as quickly as possible to liberalize all prices, privatize all state property, and stabilize their currencies, before the old communist nomenklatura could mount a political comeback. Western advisors understood that there would be resistance to these policies from "unreformed" sectors of the former planned economy, as well as economic pain for those working at uncompetitive industries and farms. They simply assumed that these negative effects of macroeconomic reform would be relatively short in duration, followed by a return to sustainable economic growth on a new market-friendly basis.[11]

The triad of price liberalization, property privatization, and currency stabilization became popularly known – and derided – as the "shock therapy" program. Did "shock therapy" directly cause the anti-Western backlash in Russia and other post-communist states? Here it is important to dispel several misunderstandings. First and foremost, the deep post-communist economic crisis, involving double-digit unemployment rates, very high rates of inflation, and massive economic dislocation in just about every country within the former Soviet bloc, was caused by the collapse of the Stalinist economic system. No simple policy formula could have prevented it. There was no gentle "evolutionary" path by which one could have magically transformed the massive, inefficient factories and farms of the planned economy into modern, globally competitive capitalist enterprises. For the Russian Federation, which inherited the very core of the old Soviet planning system, the resulting social disruption was bound to be particularly intense. In fact, the early stages of Russia's economic collapse and stealing of state assets began well before the formal collapse of the USSR, when capitalist "shock therapy" was not yet on the agenda.[12]

In addition, if you ask those involved in the economic reform effort today if they still defend "shock therapy" in Russia, they will inevitably retort that shock therapy was never actually tried there. Yeltsin's first acting prime minister, the genuinely committed liberal reformer Yegor Gaidar, did liberalize prices for most consumer goods in the wake of the Soviet collapse – a smart move, since it resulted in the quick return of foodstuffs and other basic goods to empty Russian store shelves in early 1992 – but this was not accompanied by currency stabilization of any kind. Instead, the Russian Central Bank continued to churn out rubles to provide subsidies to Russian factories and farms under distress, with the inevitable result of near hyperinflation by 1993. Moreover, the post-Soviet privatization of state property proceeded in a haphazard manner, with key state assets in the energy and minerals sectors grabbed by rapacious bosses and political insiders, while major export monopolies such as the natural gas company Gazprom remained firmly under state control. Advocates of the Washington Consensus thus say that they tried to give the right advice to their Russian colleagues, but this advice simply wasn't followed.

What this complacent analysis ignores is that actual "shock therapy" in the post-Soviet Russian context was not only never fully implemented; it was also impossible. It was one thing to try to quickly liberalize prices, privatize property, and stabilize currencies in the much smaller countries of East-Central Europe, which had only lived under communist control for about forty years, which still had a greater share of private property than the former Soviet Republics, and which were much closer to the markets and investors of Western Europe. Even in relatively well-positioned countries like Poland, the Czech Republic, and Hungary, efforts to implement "shock therapy" led to widespread anger and resentment, with long-term political effects that are still being played out. In Russia, emerging out of more than seven decades of near-total Leninist party control, inheriting a Soviet-style economy with well over 90 percent state ownership of property, and with few links to developed market economies, no politician who actually tried to fully implement the provisions of the Washington Consensus would have survived politically for long. Simply put, a sudden and complete end to all Russian state subsidies to struggling farms and factories would have meant unemployment for tens of millions of people, practically overnight. Those who say that "shock therapy was never tried" in Russia forget that advice that can't realistically be implemented is still bad advice. If you tell someone trying to escape the sheriff's posse that the best option is to jump over the Grand Canyon, you do bear some responsibility when the person who listened to your advice falls off a cliff. Nor will it comfort his grieving widow to explain: "I told him to jump *all the way over* the canyon, not stop halfway!"

Given that genuine "shock therapy" reform policies were utterly unrealistic, the West's constant repetition of the nostrums of the Washington Consensus did quite a bit of political damage. The end result of the West's celebration of Russia's faltering attempts at liberalization, privatization, and stabilization was that ordinary Russians certainly did *think* that they had suffered under Western style "shock therapy" in the 1990s. Russian workers, farmers, and professionals, after all, weren't trained in the nuances of macroeconomic theory. They had to judge the results of promised economic reforms through their personal experience. They saw that prices were freed in early 1992 – and then immediately skyrocketed to absurd levels over the next two years. In 1993, they witnessed a much-heralded process of "privatization" of state assets by means of "vouchers" given to every man, woman, and child in Russia degenerate into a corrupt asset grab by people with good political connections and few ethical principles. They breathed a sigh of relief when a belated effort at currency stabilization after 1995 appeared to tame inflation in the mid-1990s, only to watch with horror as cash-poor Soviet enterprises increasingly began paying workers with IOUs and company products instead of rubles. When the entire Russian banking system nearly collapsed for a second time in 1998, the inescapable conclusion for most Russian citizens was that the West must have been trying all along to weaken Russia through its bad economic advice.[13]

The dogmatic repetition of the mantra of liberalization, privatization, and stabilization by Western advisors to

Russia in the 1990s thus did play a significant role in undermining popular support for liberalism and democracy in the country – not because "shock therapy" caused the post-Soviet economic crisis, but because the clueless promotion of inappropriate economic formulae by the West inadvertently made economic reformers look responsible for Russia's disastrous economic performance. In the heady early days of the end of the Cold War, of course, it would have taken a great deal of foresight and self-reflection for Western politicians to tone down their triumphalism and tell their Russian partners the truth: that recovery from Stalinist misdevelopment would take decades at best. They could then have reassured the Russian leadership that the West would be there to support the Russian people on the path forward when that support was most needed. Such foresight and self-reflection, unfortunately, was almost entirely absent.

Even worse, by the end of the 1990s, jaded by the repeated disasters in Russian economic policymaking, Western opinion leaders mostly moved on to other concerns. Instead of maintaining focus on the single most significant geopolitical opportunity in a generation – to try to transform the entire northern hemisphere into a zone of peace, security, and cooperation by including Russia within the global liberal order – the West collectively turned its attention with bipartisan enthusiasm toward a different newly emerging power, China. The dwindling group of committed Russian liberal reformers watched with dismay as the same economic agencies that had promoted the Washington Consensus now bent over backwards to try to help China – still a communist one-party regime – gain entry into the World Trade Organization, from which Russia itself, notwithstanding its painful efforts to dismantle Soviet central planning, was still excluded as a "non-market economy."[14]

After the horrific 9/11 al-Qaeda terrorist attacks in New York and Washington, in which nearly 3,000 people were killed, attention shifted to the Middle East, and there was little remaining public interest in following Russian affairs. Those of us in the field of Russian Studies at the time had to fight hard to convince university administrators, donors, and foundations that it was still worth maintaining funding for our research. The consensus among pundits and policy wonks was, as a memorable headline in *The Atlantic* put it, that "Russia is finished." If Americans even saw images of Russians on their television screens as the new millennium dawned, they were likely to be characters playing incompetent mafia bosses or laughable old communists. This palpable disrespect for Russian culture also played a role in turning the majority of the Russian population against the global liberal order.[15]

* * *

We are now in a position to understand the initial appeal to broad swaths of the Russian population of the machismo and swagger of Yeltsin's designated successor, former KGB Colonel Vladimir Putin. Spoiler alert: Putin's rise to unparalleled power has nothing whatsoever to do with "deep-seated authoritarianism" within Russian culture. After all, the Russians themselves had helped to bring down the tyrannical Soviet regime, and they had initially approached the new Russian democratic order with genuine enthusiasm. But a decade of unremitting economic decline, political chaos, and cultural disruption took an inevitable toll on Russian support for democratic institutions. By the latter part of the 1990s, the word "democrat" itself became something of a swear word in Russian.

On August 16, 1999, when the ailing President Boris Yeltsin announced that the previously obscure Putin would be his new prime minister and his political "heir," Putin's popularity ratings were in the single digits. He appeared at that point to be just another grey, transitory figure taking a short turn as Yeltsin's number two, only to be discarded just like the four previous prime ministers in the year and a half before him. Putin faced a daunting array of powerful potential enemies, including Russia's ultrawealthy "oligarchs," a relatively open muckraking media, and the Fatherland–All Russia coalition, a new political party uniting the popular former Prime Minister Yevgeny Primakov, Moscow Mayor Yuri Luzhkov, and many of Russia's most important regional governors. That Putin succeeded in subordinating all of these potential opposition forces within a few years can be attributed to two factors: the outbreak of a second war with the rebellious republic of Chechnya and the dramatic recovery of the Russian economy. Together, the coincidence of these two developments meant that Putin's timing in reaching the pinnacle of power could not have been more fortunate – for him, although not for Russia and the rest of the world.[16]

After Boris Yeltsin's first attempt to subdue Chechnya militarily ended in a stalemate in 1996, the Chechen Republic was left in a state of semi-independence for the next three years. During this period, the Islamist extremist Shamil Basayev used Chechnya as a base of operations to build his personal power and to plot terrorist attacks against the Russian Federation. When he and his ally Khattab invaded the neighboring region of Dagestan on August 7, 1999, along with around two thousand troops, renewed conflict could no longer be avoided. Yeltsin appointed Putin as prime minister just over a week later.

Then, in early September, a series of apartment bombings in several Russian cities killed hundreds of innocent civilians. Although Putin blamed these terrorist attacks on the Chechens, both Chechnya's President Aslan

Maskhadov and Shamil Basayev himself denied responsibility. On September 22, local police officers in the Russian city of Ryazan caught Federal Security Service (FSB) agents placing bags of explosives in the basement of a building similar to others that had been targeted. This was dismissed as a mere "training exercise" by Putin's successor as FSB director, his close friend Nikolai Patrushev, but suspicions persist that the FSB itself may have plotted against Russian citizens themselves to create an even more dramatic pretext for war. Few Russians at the time were willing to believe such a horrible theory, however. Any discussion of the topic within Russia is now forbidden, and Patrushev has remained firmly ensconced within Putin's inner circle.[17]

Wherever precise responsibility for Russia's apartment bombings may lie, Putin took full advantage of the political opportunity to generate a "rally around the flag" effect. He now declared that the crushing of the Chechen "bandits" was his "historical mission," memorably telling journalists that if he found them on the toilet, he would "waste them in the outhouse." The Russia military began an all-out assault on Chechnya that included the carpet bombing of its capital, Grozny, with tens of thousands of civilian casualties. Russia's antiwar movement soon found itself marginalized, as a wave of patriotic sentiment spread through Russian society.[18]

At the same time as Russia's renewed military assault on Chechnya contributed to Putin's soaring political popularity, the Russian economy finally began to recover from its prolonged post-Soviet collapse. The financial crisis of 1998, which had brought down much of the Russian banking system for a second time, turned out to be the nadir of the post-Soviet Russian economic recession. By this time, the most decrepit Stalinist enterprises and farms had ceased to operate, and those with realistic economic prospects, particularly in the energy and minerals sectors, had at last restructured their operations. With the ruble now devalued, Russian consumers found it more difficult to purchase products imported from abroad, which gave a boost to domestic industry and agriculture. Even more fortuitously for Russia, the price of oil began to climb rapidly from its lows of just under $10 a barrel. Already by December 1999, oil had reached more than $26 a barrel; by the end of Putin's first term as president in 2004, it reached $40 a barrel; and by the end of his second term, oil prices reached their all-time high of $147 a barrel. As billions of dollars from energy and mineral exports began to flow into Russian state coffers, Russians watched as old Soviet buildings were finally restored and repainted, new luxury malls were opened, and trendy restaurants and cafés popped up in cities across the country. Most importantly, workers began to receive their pay on time, in rubles, instead of months late in the form of IOUs as during the late Yeltsin era.[19]

Putin's skyrocketing popularity in the first years of his reign should thus hardly be surprising. His predecessor Boris Yeltsin was visibly ailing and frequently inebriated in public. Putin came to power as a healthy 47-year-old black belt in judo who rarely drank. During the previous decade, Russia had gone from being the core of a superpower to a global laughingstock that couldn't even defeat a poor, rebellious province. Putin now pledged to make Russia a great power again. Most importantly, ordinary Russians had spent a decade coping with a devastating economic crisis, while Putin's rise to the presidency coincided with a powerful rebound in GDP that persisted throughout the 2000s. All of these factors quickly translated into rising electoral support. Putin's hastily formed Unity party gained 24 percent of the vote in the December 1999 elections, easily besting the Fatherland–All Russia group – at least according to the official electoral figures – and he cruised to victory in the presidential elections of March 2000 with the support of over 53 percent of Russian voters.[20]

Having succeeded unexpectedly in gaining control over the Russian government, Putin now pledged to his exhausted populace that he would restore the power of the Russian state. No objective analyst could possibly have quarreled with this priority. A decade of post-Soviet state weakness had produced nothing but misery, deprivation, and defeat for Russian society. Even many Western policymakers, having witnessed the repeated failures of Russia's efforts at market reform, greeted Putin's state-building project with relief and approval.

Unfortunately, Putin's model for state-building was from the beginning patrimonial in essence, rather than oriented toward the rule of law. Many Western analysts, accustomed to thinking of "the state" and "the market" as a simple dichotomy, misunderstood the fundamentally traditional elements of Putin's conception of the state. When Putin demanded a restoration of what he called "the vertical of power" in Russian politics, he did not have in mind the creation of well-functioning modern administrative agencies. He did expand employment in state agencies as compared to the Yeltsin era, it is true – but he did not manage to consolidate a modern civil service system. Instead, he rebuilt the Russian state primarily by relying on friends and colleagues with whom he had longstanding relations of personal trust to carry out his orders, who in turn promoted their own cronies and relatives to influential state positions.

Putin's deep personal loyalty to his closest friends and long-time associates is one of the most striking features of his approach to politics. Nearly a quarter century after he came to power, he continued to surround himself with many of the same men – and practically no women – he first met in the late Soviet and early post-Soviet periods. Certainly, his oldest friends have benefited handsomely from their close association with him. As a teenager growing up in Leningrad (as Saint Petersburg was called in Soviet times), Putin took self-defense classes with the brothers Arkady and Boris Rotenberg, initiating a lifelong bond. Putin rewarded the Rotenberg brothers' loyalty by elevating them to leadership positions in one of Russia's major construction companies; today, they are both billionaires. And when Putin needed a favor in return – namely, the building of a new bridge linking the Russian mainland to the annexed Ukrainian Crimean peninsula – the Rotenberg brothers were only too happy to volunteer their company's services. Sergei Roldugin, a professional cellist who has known Putin since the 1970s, is now a multimillionaire, a financial status that obviously owes more to his role in helping Putin smuggle Russian state assets into hidden offshore accounts than it does to his musical prowess.[21]

Beyond loyalty to his oldest friends, Putin's political career put him in the "right place at the right time" to forge personal bonds with powerful cliques within Russia's security services as well as with well-known advocates of market reform. He thus managed to appeal simultaneously to those who wanted a "tough guy" to take the reins of power, and to Russian liberals who thought that a strong state was needed to modernize the Russian economy in the face of social opposition. Remarkably, Putin remained loyal to associates within both camps, despite all their differences, throughout his reign.

As a KGB colonel who had been recruited for the Soviet spy agency in the 1970s, Putin got to know others in the intelligence and security services who shared his conspiratorial and cynical view of the West and of post-Soviet "democratization" alike, particularly colleagues within the Leningrad KGB hierarchy, such as Nikolai Patrushev, Alexander Bortnikov, and Sergei Naryshkin. As of 2023,

Patrushev was leading Putin's powerful Security Council; Bortnikov was directing the FSB, the main successor to the KGB; and Naryshkin was heading up Russia's foreign intelligence service. All three remained key advisors to the president as he prosecuted his bloody war in Ukraine. Putin also hit it off with Sergei Shoigu, who served in the 1990s as Yeltsin's minister for emergency situations, the equivalent of the US Federal Emergency Management Agency. Putin trusted Shoigu enough to make him official first leader of Putin's Unity Party in 1999 and to appoint him, ultimately, as minister of defense, despite the fact that he had no real military training or experience.

After the collapse of the Soviet Union, Putin was hired as the Deputy Mayor of Saint Petersburg under Mayor Anatoly Sobchak, considered a liberal reformer at the time. In this role, Putin rubbed shoulders with key figures among Russia's emerging liberal elite, including Dmitry Medvedev, German Gref, and Alexei Kudrin. Medvedev became Putin's prime minister and even took the role of Russia's president from 2008 to 2012; he was eventually appointed deputy chair of the Security Council and became a histrionic ultra-hawk concerning the war in Ukraine. Gref has been the head of Sberbank, one of Russia's largest financial institutions, since 2007. Kudrin was brought into Putin's government as minister of finance from 2000 to 2011; Kudrin later headed up Russia's central auditing agency until 2022. One other crony from Putin's days in Sobchak's mayoral administration remained especially powerful: Viktor Zolotov, Putin's bodyguard since the early 1990s, who was appointed in 2016 as head of the newly formed Russian National Guard, a military force of some 350,000 men.

Overall, as one would expect in a patrimonial regime, there was remarkably little turnover within Putin's ruling "family" over time. A few of Putin's former close colleagues have gone into retirement – still enjoying the lucrative spoils of their state service – but almost no one in his inner circle has ever decided to betray him openly. Of course, such deference to Putin by his close associates makes perfect sense, given the two options available to these people: either to enjoy riches beyond most of our imaginations in perpetuity by remaining loyal, or to face almost certain death for open disloyalty. The damaging consequences of rule by Putin's extended household since 1999 have been similar to those caused by the aging of the Soviet Communist Party elite under Leonid Brezhnev. Russia's government has increasingly become a sclerotic gerontocracy, and slots within the top elite for new people with new ideas are correspondingly limited.

The most notable exception to this pattern of mutual loyalty within the president's inner circle only proves the rule. When Putin's longtime close associate Yevgeny Prigozhin decided to launch a military mutiny in June 2023 against Minister of Defense Shoigu and Chief of the General Staff Valery Gerasimov, whom he accused of gross incompetence in leading Russia's military efforts in Ukraine, he took care never to criticize Putin directly by name. For a few weeks, it looked as if this formal deference to the boss might have saved Prigozhin from the dismal fate of other opposition figures – until a suspiciously timed plane crash in August killed him and two of his top lieutenants.

Putin's apologists have tended to excuse his autocratic tendencies by claiming that at least his dictatorship has brought measurable improvements to the Russian public. Indeed, as even objective analysis has shown, during Putin's first two terms in office from 2000 to 2008 the Russian state undeniably did perform better than it had under the drunken, mercurial Yeltsin. Russia's formal legal code was strengthened, and its tax collection system was streamlined and rationalized. Russia ran repeated government budget surpluses, and, by 2006, the country had proudly paid off all its remaining Soviet-era foreign debt. It helped that Putin's inner circle included not only old judo partners and intelligence agents, but also competent technocrats he had met in the early post-Soviet era.[22]

So why didn't Putin's Russia become another Singapore? Like all patrimonial regimes, Putin's Russia gradually but inexorably corroded from the rot of cronyism and corruption. The logical corollary of building a state based above all on personal loyalty to the ruler is that open disloyalty must be ruthlessly punished. And over time, Putin's regime relied on increasingly brutal coercion to maintain control. At first, mostly those with the temerity to organize openly against the regime were attacked. Oppositional billionaires like Vladimir Gusinsky and Mikhail Khodorkovsky were jailed, stripped of their business and media empires, and exiled – the latter after serving a brutal ten-year prison sentence in Siberia. Regional governors who had ruled independently of the Kremlin through their own local machines were brought to heel. Chechnya was finally bombed into submission, with Putin loyalist Ramzan Kadyrov installed as a "mini-Putin" to manage the rebellious republic. Investigative journalist Anna Politkovskaya was gunned down in the elevator of her apartment block, while Aleksandr Litvinenko, a prominent defector from the Russian intelligence services, died after drinking radioactive poisoned tea.[23]

Yet during the 2000s, some scope still remained for nongovernmental organizations to criticize Russian government policies, defend marginalized groups in Russian society, and even expose instances of official corruption and malfeasance. In this period, Putin still liked to think of himself as a "constitutional" leader – even if his regime manipulated elections at every level to ensure the desired results. His remarkable decision to become Russia's prime minister and let his loyal subordinate Dmitry Medvedev switch places with him as president from 2008 until 2012, rather than formally abrogate the Russian Constitution's two-term limit for the presidency, can only be explained in this light.

The deeper logic of patrimonialism, however, soon overwhelmed what remained of these formal legal constraints on Putin's power. Even under Medvedev's presidency, Putin continued to make almost all the key executive decisions. And as the presidential elections of 2012 approached, Putin announced publicly not only that he would be returning to his former position, but also that he and Medvedev had planned for this switcheroo from the very beginning, infuriating millions of Russians who saw this disdain for democratic procedures as disrespectful. The open fraud committed in Russia's parliamentary elections of December 2011 to ensure a majority for the pro-regime United Russia party – much of it caught on videos shared widely on Russian social media – added fuel to the growing popular anger. Hundreds of thousands of protestors gathered for rallies in many major Russian cities, calling for a "Russia without Putin" – protests that Putin blamed on then-US Secretary of State Hillary Clinton. From this point on, Putin decided that allowing any scope whatsoever for independent political activity would only open him up to the threat of being toppled in a "color revolution" like Ukraine's 2004 Orange Revolution.[24]

Since Putin's return to the Russian presidency in 2012, the patrimonial principle has increasingly dominated political life. NGO activity that had formerly been permitted became subject to increasingly harsh penalties governing the activity of "foreign agents." The dwindling group of independent journalists was harassed, driven out of the country, or killed. Like Politkovskaya and Litvinenko, those seen as "traitors" to Putin's state at home and abroad continued to die under mysterious circumstances. Opposition politician Boris Nemtsov was gunned down not far from the Kremlin – supposedly by rogue Chechens – in 2015. Anti-corruption crusader Aleksei Navalny was poisoned with the nerve agent Novichok, receiving urgent medical care in Germany; he boldly returned to Russia, only to be rearrested and sent to his death in a maximum-security prison.

Not coincidentally, the escalation of state repression was accompanied by ever more grandiose declarations of love for and loyalty to Putin by his cronies and sycophants. Building on the official cult of personality developed early in Putin's reign, state-controlled media now depicted him helping endangered young cranes navigate the Siberian skies from his hang-glider and camping bare-chested in the forest, taking a dip in an icy lake. Putin also grew ever closer to reactionary Patriarch Kirill of the Russian Orthodox Church, who called Putin's rule a "miracle of God." By 2014, after Putin's annexation of what he now termed the "holy land" of Crimea, along with military incursions into Eastern Ukraine, speaker of the State Duma Vyacheslav Volodin could proudly proclaim: "Without Putin, there is no Russia." A more succinct summary of the patrimonial essence of the Putin regime can hardly be imagined. Thus, it was no surprise in the summer of 2020 when Russian voters in a sham referendum approved amendments to the Russian Constitution allowing Putin to serve as president for an additional two six-year presidential terms – that is, until 2036, by which time he would be 83 years old.[25]

Inevitably, as in all patrimonial regimes, the shrinking space for independent initiative and autonomy within the Russian state undermined its ability to ensure economic dynamism and to provide public goods. Since 2008, when the global price of oil peaked, the Russian economy has stagnated, growing at about 1 percent a year on average. The corruption of Russian state officialdom means that construction managers can ignore safety regulations easily by paying a few bribes, with the inevitable result of needless civilian deaths in devastating fires and building collapses. Russia's performance during the COVID-19 pandemic was among the worst in the world, with Putin leaving the public health response largely to regional governors while he himself stayed in strict isolation, forcing visitors to wait for weeks before meeting with him – and even then, only at the other end of a very long table. And under the veneer of a vaunted "modernization" program, Russia's military readiness has decayed through mismanagement by corrupt generals and the ongoing brutal hazing of poorly trained recruits.

Putin's unprovoked full-scale invasion of Ukraine in February 2022 finally roused complacent Western elites and educated publics from the comforting illusion that Russia could be safely ignored. It also laid bare the inner rot of the Russian state. Instead of marching to an easy victory, the Russian military became bogged down in a bloody quagmire from which there was no easy escape. Hundreds of thousands of Russia's best and brightest young workers have fled the country to avoid conscription and deployment at the front, including many of those who represented the future of the once-promising Russian tech industry. Internal security is so weak that when Prigozhin decided to launch a "march for justice" against the Russian high command, he was able to seize the Russian Southern Military District command without firing a shot and then march to within a couple of hundred miles of Moscow. Fear prevents Russians from answering public opinion polls honestly, but underneath Putin's official sky-high popularity, doubt and uncertainty about the future is growing. Yet as the Russian war on Ukraine approached its third year, Putin remained confident that time was on his side, as the diffusion of his patrimonial model of rule throughout the world continued to undermine the cohesion of the Western alliance opposing the invasion of Ukraine. Terrifyingly, Putin's prediction may yet be proven correct.

5

The Wave: From East to West

Why did Matteo Salvini, leader of the far-right Italian political party The League, choose to wear a T-shirt with an image of Putin in military gear during a trip to Red Square in Moscow in 2015? Why did the American rightwing Conservative Political Action Conference (CPAC) choose to hold annual meetings in Budapest, Hungary, with Putin admirer Viktor Orbán as a featured speaker in 2022 and 2023? Why was Nigel Farage, leader of the UK Independence Party that championed Brexit, spotted in Mississippi campaigning for Donald Trump in 2016? And why did Benjamin Netanyahu emulate Orbán in moving to weaken Israel's independent judiciary, while copying Donald Trump's tactic of blaming all opposition to his personal rule on the deep state? The answer in brief: what started in Russia did not stay in Russia. We tend to think that political innovation moves from the West to the East and the South; that is, everyone imitates the West. But this isn't always the case. The untold story of the past decade has been the spread of traditional modes of personalist rule from Russia to the West. In various shapes and sizes, the patrimonial assault on the modern state diffused to countries as diverse as Ukraine, Hungary, Israel, the UK, and the United States. But how and why did this occur?[1]

It is tempting to blame everything on Russian machinations. Certainly, Putin's regime has sought to export his model of governance, especially within its immediate geopolitical neighborhood, but also well beyond. Part of the story undoubtedly is Russian support for kindred parties and movements abroad, financed by oil and gas exports. We still don't know the full scope of Russia's efforts to shape governments around the world, including the backing of anti-establishment social movements, the organization of mass influence operations on social media, and, on occasion, the outright purchasing of politicians. That the Kremlin has deliberately and consistently worked to undermine liberalism in countries throughout the world, however, is by now undeniable.

Even so, Russian influence would not have amounted to much had the ground not already been well prepared for it. An equally important part of the story, then, are the economic and social conditions that brought the modern state into disrepute, making Putin's patrimonial model appear for many to be an effective and appealing alternative. Throughout the world, a loose coalition of anti-state libertarians, religious nationalists, and supporters of unabashed executive power has worked to undermine the administrative agencies and legal bodies that make the modern state function. The precise admixture of political forces involved varies from country to country, of course, depending on local conditions. But the overall pattern is clear.

Patrimonialism was easiest to reinforce in the post-Soviet region, where personalistic rule was in many places a direct legacy of the communist past. Former communist bosses in Central Asia and the Caucasus quickly transformed themselves into "democrats," and then just as quickly reinvented themselves again as autocratic "fathers" of their nations. In these post-Soviet states, impersonal state structures mostly did not need to be dismantled, because they did not yet exist. And as the most powerful boss in a world of post-Soviet bosses, Putin naturally emerged as the *primus inter pares*.

Had it not been for the global financial crisis that began in 2008, however, Putin's reinforcement of personalistic rulers might have been confined to Eurasia. Instead, the global collapse of housing markets, massive recession, and soaring inequality fundamentally discredited both the Washington Consensus and the leaders who had supported it. The "losers" of neoliberal globalization – workers in dying blue-collar towns, marginalized rural populations, and supporters of traditional values – now mobilized in countries around the world against the "corrupt elites" who had seemingly benefited unfairly from pell-mell marketization. Few noticed at the time that this was precisely the same social coalition that had supported Putin's destruction of oligarchs, opposition parties, and liberal civil society in Russia after 2000.

The virus of patrimonialism thus spread unexpectedly to every part of the world. In Hungary and other new EU member states, where huge efforts had been put into creating modern regulatory regimes, leaders bit the European hand that fed them. In Israel, a country that placed statehood at the core of its identity, Benjamin Netanyahu's assault on the order in search of personal aggrandizement and protection from prosecution culminated in an attempted "judicial coup." In the UK, Boris Johnson not only took his county out of the EU, but his successors also took aim at "Big Everything" – especially Britain's regulatory state. And Donald Trump transformed the United States into the new epicenter of the global assault on the modern state by vilifying virtually every public institution in the country.

The assault on the modern state has not yet destroyed it, but it has generated a global struggle between two principles of rule – in short, the rule of law versus the rule of men – the outcome of which has yet to be decided.

* * *

Russia's attack on Ukraine in February 2022 unleashed a debate in the West about the Kremlin's war aims. What did Vladimir Putin want? As Russia's forces mercilessly targeted Ukrainian civilians, reduced Ukrainian cities to rubble, and littered the country with deadly landmines, debates about Putin's ultimate motivations reached fever pitch. But the simple dichotomy driving many of these debates – namely, that Putin is either "crazy" or a "rational actor" – was fundamentally misleading. This framing of the issue sheds little insight into the type of regime Putin had built in Russia, nor does it pinpoint the broader social forces within the country that have sustained the regime during the conflict.

Instead, we need to understand Russia's foreign policy as intimately connected with the personalistic regime now ruling the country. Having crushed opposition forces within Russia that Putin perceived as traitorously pro-Western, Putin set out to make global geopolitics safe for patrimonialism. In short: what Putin wanted was a world run by other Putins. Within the territory he considered historically part of the Russian imperium, he wanted patrimonial leaders willing to pledge fealty to him personally. This was quickly accomplished in Russia's provinces. Even in the erstwhile separatist Chechnya, Putin installed mini-Putin Ramzan Kadyrov, the son of an assassinated separatist leader who officially became "president" when he reached 30, the minimum age for the executive under the Chechen constitution. Kadyrov proceeded to construct his own tiny and violent despotic regime, including typical patrimonial flourishes such as his personal menagerie of black swans, bears, lions, and tigers, to whom he had threatened to feed independent journalists and political opponents – who in any case had a bad habit of disappearing.[2]

Outside Russia, Putin's foreign policy challenges could be more complex, but the task of cementing patrimonial alliances was nevertheless manageable. Consider Kazakhstan. Born out of the Soviet collapse, without a cohesive national identity, and with a large ethnic Russian and Russian-speaking population, Kazakhstan was ruled until 2019 by Nursultan Nazarbayev, an ethnic Kazakh and one-time steel worker whom Gorbachev had made head of the republic's communist party. Refashioning himself as a Central Asian potentate, Nazarbayev and his family ruled the country through a mix of tyranny, oil wealth, and crony capitalism. The major new investments made by Western energy companies and the promise of new connections to China gave Nazarbayev significant room for maneuver – but nevertheless, Putin and Nazarbayev fundamentally operated according to the same political rules, with both understanding Putin's primacy in their personal relationship.

A similar pattern emerged in Belarus under former collective farm chairman President Aliaksandr Lukashenka. Having come to power in 1994, after the failure of "shock therapy" in Russia was already apparent, Lukashenka declined to privatize Belarus's economy. The class of oligarchs that appeared in Russia after 1991 thus failed to materialize, and Lukashenka was free to build his own personalistic "vertical of power." In effect, he became his own oligarch. Casting himself as the Belarusians' virile local father who loved nothing more than working the land, bringing in the harvest together with beautiful women, doling out goods to favored cronies, and staffing his country's bureaucracy and judiciary with sycophants, Lukashenka fit the patrimonial mold. As in the case of Kazakhstan, Lukashenka created some wiggle room for independent action from Russia by exploring closer ties with Europe and China, but Putin remained the dominant figure in Russian–Belarussian relations – particularly after Lukashenka was forced to rely on Russian support to put down massive antiregime protests after the sham presidential elections of 2020. In 2022, Lukashenka allowed his country to be used as a staging ground for Russia's war against Ukraine and in 2023 as a temporary refuge for Putin's not-always-loyal private army, PMC Wagner.[3]

It's tempting to understand these developments as Putin's effort to recreate the old Soviet Union. But this would be inaccurate. Like Nazarbayev, Lukashenka sometimes successfully resisted the embrace of the Slavic big brother when it threatened his image and clan power. This was not quite the old Soviet Union with its uniform ideology, strongly institutionalized one-party rule, and strict subordination to Moscow. The proper imagery is more like the "heads of families" in Mario Puzo's *The Godfather*, working out problems, divvying up the spoils, sometimes quarreling, but helping each other when needed. Putin in this scheme occupied the position of the *capo di tutti capi*, the boss of bosses – in short, the big man.[4]

Ukraine's wartime president, Volodymyr Zelenskyy, was quite the other thing. He first came on the national scene in 2015 through his television show *The Servant of the People*, which ran for three seasons. In it, Zelenskyy plays an underpaid high school history teacher, Vasily Goloborodko, who lives with his parents and becomes president almost by accident. In a bitter rant to a colleague at school, Goloborodko confides his true feelings about the country's self-serving political class. Unbeknownst to him, a student secretly records it, posts it online, and the clip goes viral during election season. He wakes up the morning after the election to find himself president, surrounded by sycophants and all the temptations of power. The entire series revolves around the modest, self-critical "little man" – the anti-Putin – confronting a corrupt and inefficient state that remains proudly democratic but strains to provide most public services, while other state officials and unseen oligarchs work to undermine his efforts. It's light fare but captures something of the state-builder's dilemma.[5]

In a truly remarkable historical twist, Zelenskyy himself was indeed propelled into the presidency in 2019, heading up a new political party named after his television show. Why, then, did Ukraine not become another Belarus? Putin wanted this and it may still occur in at least part of the country if Moscow gets its way. Yet a central feature of Ukrainian politics and society has prevented the consolidation of patrimonial rule: its remarkably powerful civic national identity. Although Ukraine emerged as a newly independent state as a result of the Soviet collapse, the country's nation-building project is old and well established, both within the country and among the highly active Ukrainian diaspora. And even as serious disagreements about how to define "Ukrainian-ness" sometimes hamper unity and provide grist for politicians seeking to divide the population, even before the full-scale Russian invasion in 2022 the vast majority of Ukrainians were keen to distance themselves from Putin's project. Many Ukrainians speak Russian as their native tongue, most of them fluently, but very few wanted to integrate into Putin's world.

Ukraine's firm sense of national identity has prevented would-be Putins from replicating his successful effort to establish a single "vertical of power" in the country. As a result, before the full-scale Russian invasion of 2022, Ukrainian politics looked a lot more like Yeltsin's chaotic regime in the 1990s than like Putin's dictatorship. Unlike Russia in 1991, Ukraine initially postponed privatization. But in 1994, under its second president, Leonid Kuchma, the country ultimately sold off state assets and created a large class of fabulously wealthy oligarchs. Some were connected to Kuchma personally, such as his son-in-law Viktor Pinchuk, but others, such as the "gas princess" Yulia Tymoshenko, Putin crony Viktor Medvedchuk, and Zelenskyy's early patron Igor Kolomoisky, were almost "accidental" multimillionaires and billionaires. These winners of privatization colonized the state, some becoming governors or heads of ministries that regulated the same industries they controlled, others becoming members of parliament to secure the immunity from prosecution this bestowed. Kuchma failed to create a single chain of command subordinated to him personally, yielding what one scholar has termed "pluralism by default." This failure to consolidate personalistic rule kept the country democratic – but it also yielded a corrupt and feeble state that frequently failed to pay its civil servants, pave its roads, tax its population, regulate its banks and industry, or enforce the rule of law.[6]

Kuchma's decision to decentralize wealth through corrupt privatization of state assets also meant that his oligarchic supporters became independent enough to throw their support to other candidates. This is exactly what occurred in the runup to the presidential election of 2004, when a critical mass of oligarchs withdrew their support from Viktor Yanukovych, Kuchma's handpicked successor. Raised in the hardscrabble Donbas, the burly, Russian-speaking politician with the overly sprayed mafia boss hairdo seemed drawn from central casting. Twice convicted for assault and robbery in his youth, he landed in the trucking industry and then in provincial administration in Donetsk. When his opponent, Viktor Yushchenko, who had served as Kuchma's central bank head, fell gravely ill from dioxin poisoning during the campaign, suspicion fell immediately on the Yanukovych campaign: poisoning was the Russian FSB's modus operandi, after all.

On election day Yanukovych prevailed, but fraudulently, sparking widespread public protests and a cascade of oligarchic defection to Yushchenko. In the subsequent rerun of the vote, Yushchenko was declared the winner. The "Orange Revolution," as the events of fall 2004 were dubbed, resulted from a combination of civic mobiliz-ation and oligarchic machinations that showed the limits of presidential power in Ukraine – for pro-Russian and pro-Western presidents alike. Yushchenko may have been a "Westernizer," but in the post-Orange Revolution years of his presidency the state remained ineffectual and corrupt, the plaything of the oligarchs. One former official working on infrastructure projects interviewed for this book told of bribery, large and small, so commonplace that it attracted no attention; he himself was passed an envelope of cash worth a month's salary simply for taking a meeting with a lobbyist, with no expectation of quid pro quo in the short run. He further noted the lack of any collaboration among "teams" of officials tied either to Yushchenko, Tymoshenko, or Yanukovych. They simply refused to attend each other's meetings, wary of being seen as working with or for another patron. Most crucially, he noted, the constant rise and fall of ruling coalitions, along with the penetration of the state by private money, made it impossible to plan for the long run: "Don't plan on being here more than a month," he was told. Yushchenko never managed to build a Western-style bureaucracy, but he also failed to construct a unified personal "vertical of power." As his popularity waned, he retreated into identity politics, which in Ukraine inevitably divided the country regionally along linguistic and cultural lines and raised the thorny and essentially unresolvable questions of local collaboration in past eras with the Soviet and Nazi dictatorships.

Paul Manafort, the American consultant who ultimately became Donald Trump's campaign chair, worked on Yanukovych's political makeover. The two men even started to resemble each other, as a master begins to resemble his dog. Paid by oligarchs close to Putin, Manafort describes in his memoirs how Yanukovych's political party, the Party of Regions, strategized to take advantage of regional polarization around language and history: "The Party of Regions used the anti-eastern Ukraine slant of the Yushchenko government as a rallying point for building political support in the east ... This was a growing issue in 2005 in Ukraine. Yanukovych's rivals ... were trying to delegitimize Russian culture in Ukraine in order to rid the nation of feelings that they falsely claimed were dangerous to uniting the country."[7] Remarkably, the same set of players who initially supported the Ukrainian patrimonial state-building project later reemerged as part of Trump's attempt to subvert the US legal state.

But in the short run, at least, Manafort's advice worked. In 2010, Yanukovych won a relatively clean presidential election against his opponent, Yulia Tymoshenko, the gas princess. He and those around him had learned an important lesson from the Orange Revolution, however. Retaining power required the construction of a Russian-style personalized power vertical, something no Ukrainian president had yet accomplished. There were too many oligarchs with access to state power, and no president could count on their support. Setting out to rectify matters, Yanukovych's people first attacked the older generation of grandees. Tymoshenko was imprisoned and became in effect Ukraine's Mikhail Khodorkovsky, a warning to an entire generation not to cross the new boss. Yanukovych's son, also called Viktor, did not occupy any formal office, but he maneuvered with his father's help to place his personal friends in ministerial positions, a coterie he then tried to sell to the West as a team of "young reformers," because they were mostly in their thirties. This group spearheaded the project of redistributing wealth from the older oligarchs to new ones. Those among the older generation of oligarchs who retained their riches – such as the wealthiest person in Ukraine, Rinat Akhmetov – were forced to "kiss the ring."

One prong of Yanukovych's strategy for duplicating the Russian state model entailed staffing the state elite with family and friends. Equally important was the placement of Russian agents and citizens in key security ministries, including the prosecutor general, the minister of defense, the minister of interior, and even the head of the Ukrainian Security Services, the SBU. All of these officials would either flee to Russia or be unmasked as Russian agents in 2014.

The plan for Putinism in Ukraine almost worked. It ran aground because Yanukovych could not destroy Ukrainian society's deep desire to "return to Europe" and escape the pull of Putin's regime. During his electoral campaign, Yanukovych declared his openness to an EU Association agreement that would ultimately have required a total overhaul of the country's legal system and regulatory bodies. But on the eve of an EU summit in Vilnius in November 2013, where he was about to sign the agreement, Yanukovych balked in the face of threats and bribes from Russia – specifically, the threat of an economic blockade if he signed and the promise of $15 billion in loans if he did not. According to historian Serhii Plokhy, Yanukovych also explained to his entourage that Putin had told him he would never allow the EU or NATO to expand to the Ukrainian border with Russia. If Yanukovych signed the EU agreement, Putin threatened to occupy Crimea, the

Donbas, and much of southeastern Ukraine. At the last moment, Yanukovych caved in and withdrew from signing the agreement.[8]

Ukrainian society reacted angrily and, despite bitterly cold weather, occupied the Maidan (Independence Square) in downtown Kyiv. This time, Yanukovych's government responded with violence, leading ultimately to a massacre of more than a hundred people, both on and off the main square. Although Yanukovych had completed a great deal of his patrimonial state-building project, consolidating a personalistic regime takes time – as the Russian case shows. In 2014, portions of the government, the oligarchs, and the citizenry retained enough autonomy to refuse to follow Yanukovych's orders. Rather than face his impending political downfall in Ukraine, Yanukovych fled to Russia under Putin's protection.[9]

Unable to install his personal crony in Ukraine and confident that the Americans would do little to stop him, Putin chose to launch a frontal attack on Ukraine's sovereignty. He invaded and annexed Crimea and sent in Russian troops to support separatist movements in the Donbas, marking the start of Russia's long war with Ukraine. Ukraine, however, continued bravely to resist. In the ensuing years, between 2014 and 2022, Ukraine rebuilt its military with enough capacity to forestall the realization of Putin's war plans, while holding two more free and fair presidential elections. Whether wartime solidarity will turn Ukraine away from the patrimonial state-building project once and for all, however, remains an open question. It is much harder to build a modern state based on the long-term benefits of the impersonal legal order than to distribute the short-term gains from a patrimonial regime of the type built by Putin in Russia.

* * *

The playbook for the assault on the modern state in the former Soviet republics called for killing it in its infancy. In the developed West, it has required something altogether different: demolishing an expert-led bureaucratic and regulatory apparatus, built up over decades. These bureaucracies provide an impressive range of public goods upon which the entire society depends. The irony for the new European Union member states is that the enemies of the modern state had to attack the EU itself, for it is arguably this organization that brought modern government to the region in the wake of communism's collapse.

It is now easy to forget just how powerful the allure of joining the EU was after the fall of the Berlin Wall in 1989. The acronym and symbols had become synonymous with Europe itself: the EU *was* Europe. Having regained their sovereignty after the fall of the Soviet bloc, Hungary and Poland ran as fast as they could to Brussels to relinquish it again, trying to win the lottery of history and join the West. Throughout the 1990s and early 2000s, both countries subordinated every aspect of their foreign and domestic politics to the goal of EU accession.

Emerging originally out of a coal and steel union designed to prevent war between France and Germany, the European Union evolved over time into a highly integrated economic and political bloc. With the accession of Greece in 1981 and Spain and Portugal in 1986, the EU became even more: a vehicle for democratizing and stabilizing the continent's periphery. In 1989, when the Berlin Wall fell, Spain and Portugal seemed well on their way to being Europe's California and Oregon – beautiful, democratic, and prosperous.

And it was this prospect of joining the West that created a breathless desire for EU membership among Hungary and the other former Warsaw Pact states. Europe held its doors open, but made membership conditional on passing what by the late 1990s had ballooned into 88,000 pages of EU law and regulations – known collectively as the *acquis communautaire* – into local legislation and implementing it, no questions asked. Regulations on everything ranging from economic competition to environmental regulation and even the transportation of geese were simply translated into local languages and, where necessary, passed into law in national parliaments with no debate.

Brussels offered a great deal of support, seconding teams of their own bureaucrats to ministries in every capital in East-Central Europe. The European Commission, the EU's central administrative bureaucracy, "monitored" everything, and as long as membership remained uncertain, its monitoring reports carried great weight in Central European capitals. The Commission, as one political scientist put it, was the tutor, and the Central Europeans were the pupils. Clean elections were expected, of course. But the core task of EU enlargement was not just democratization. In fact, EU expansion amounted to a big modern state-building project, replacing the militarized totalitarian leviathans of the communist world with the law-based regulatory states of the EU. Inevitably, some of this emulation remained words on paper, but a great deal of post-communist East-Central European state-building was genuine. Implementing these changes required suspending local judgments, customs, and, in some meaningful ways, sovereignty. Sometimes, it meant just keeping quiet and following orders, an irony lost on no one in former vassal states of the Soviet bloc.[10]

And therein lay the rub. EU support and guidance frequently felt more like imposition and diktat. Once the first ten new EU member states were admitted in 2004, reality set in and long-suppressed attitudes on matters ranging from nationalism to gender relations to human sexuality could be openly expressed – at first with transgressive laughter, and later with deep earnestness and, for many, repressed resentment. Nowhere did this combination of messages initially find a warmer welcome than in Viktor Orbán's Hungary, a country that confronted stiff economic headwinds after the global financial crisis of 2008, the shock of cultural modernization in the runup to and aftermath of its EU accession, and then the refugee crisis during the Syrian civil war. It was one thing for Brussels to require regulatory harmonization but, as one older conservative Hungarian man complained, "quite another to tell us how women should be women."

Orbán's genius, after he returned to power in 2010 with a parliamentary supermajority for his Fidesz party, was in asserting the patrimonial principle with trappings of formal "legality." Much attention has been devoted to his authoritarianism: his assault on the media, fiddling with the electoral system and number of seats in parliament, the use of Russian-style "political technologies" to field bogus candidates and so divide the anti-Fidesz vote, and the unceasing drumbeat of government propaganda. Equally important, however, was his assault on the state itself, subordinating the country's court system, firing civil servants *en masse*, installing personal allies in key bureaucratic positions, and melding political and economic power.

Orbán's policies amounted to a strange combination of traditionalism and kleptocracy, wrapped in a veneer of clever legalism – to the direct benefit of his cronies. Ordinarily, one would not have expected a gasfitter from the sleepy town of Felcsút to become Hungary's richest man. "God, luck, and Viktor Orbán certainly played a role in what I've achieved so far," reported Lőrinc Mészáros, the Hungarian PM's childhood friend, explaining his unprecedented business success in 2014. Three years later, Mészáros became an international business superstar for having the world's best performing stock – thanks to his steady stream of government contracts. His response to reporters who wanted to know how he had grown his business faster than Mark Zuckerberg's: "I am most likely smarter than Mark Zuckerberg."[11]

The circle of beneficiaries of the regime's corruption extended beyond front men such as Mészáros to Orbán's immediate family members, especially his father and his son-in-law István Tibor. Hungary's crony capitalism increasingly resembled the models of the ex-Soviet republics where oligarchic and political power are closely related. The difference, however, is this order was built within the EU and, in part, with EU money. Government contracts enriching Fidesz supporters come disproportionately from EU transfer funds, with part of those funds then donated back to Fidesz or to support other politically connected businesses.[12]

EU regulations designed to level the economic playing field among member states were frequently twisted to serve corrupt ends. In 2023, the country's state-friendly oil giant, MOL, eyed the profitable scrap and garbage collection business in Hungary. Using compliance gaps in EU recycling and recovery regulations – gaps the government itself had widened by eschewing recycling technology in favor of a packaging tax that flowed directly into state coffers – the oil giant convinced political leaders and relevant ministries to issue a tender for a monopoly concession. As one executive from a medium-sized scrap company told us, MOL executives were quite aware that they ran the only company in Hungary that could meet its terms, even though its prior expertise in these businesses was nonexistent. The plan was to use hundreds of existing scrap businesses as subcontractors and to skim off the profit. Industry complaints were met with silence. Some foreign scrap companies decided to leave Hungary; others sought to sell their stakes to regime-friendly oligarchs as quickly as possible.

Emblematic of the entire personalistic turn was the evolution of the so-called System of National Cooperation (NER in Hungary), which began with the idea of creating a "national" elite in an economy dependent on foreign investment. Over time, however, it amounted to a scheme for privatizing state assets and outsourcing state functions to Fidesz cronies, fittingly dubbed by the opposition as "NER-knights." In return for political loyalty, the knights received juicy chunks of state business, hefty remuneration, and positions as trustees on boards of newly created "foundations" that run cultural and higher educational institutions with high-value assets. The EU saw through part of the maneuver, withdrawing some support from universities under the control of the foundations, but could do little to unravel the entire set of policies.[13]

Although Orbán rarely spoke explicitly of the "deep state," with the help of an American political consultant he did conjure up the bogeyman of George Soros, the liberal Hungarian-American Jewish financier who supposedly schemes tirelessly to flood the country with immigrants and dilute its Christian character. Hazy allegations of a "Soros plan" to undermine Hungarian sovereignty and culture littered Hungarian political discourse, especially during election season. But Orbán's true "deep state" bogeyman always remained, ironically, the EU itself. Notwithstanding EU largesse filling his and his loyalists' pockets, Orbán regularly railed against "federalists" – that is, would-be state builders in Brussels who seek to impose their vision of civil rights and cultural relativism on the country. It is this antipathy to the formal European legal system, along with the promise of cheap energy, that brought Orbán into Putin's orbit. Russia did not "purchase" Hungarian politics in any appreciable way, but it did back selected politicians such as the leaders of Jobbik, an on-again off-again fixture of Hungary's far right, further augmenting pro-Kremlin voices in the Hungarian parliament.[14]

Orbán's regime also caught the eye of like-minded conservative intellectuals and media figures in the US and elsewhere. Orbán proudly proclaimed that Hungary's democracy was "illiberal" and "Christian," committed to the collective Hungarian nation rather than individual rights. These stances put him at odds with the EU, which, according to Orbán, had conducted an "LGBT offensive." In 2021, Fidesz passed a law prohibiting the use of materials seen as promoting "homosexuality" and "gender ideology" at schools, citing the need to protect children from "LGBTQ propaganda." Orbán's Christian conservatism, admiration for unbridled executive power, fear of immigration, willingness to criticize the US Democratic Party but never Putin, and, above all, his playbook for using legal means to attack the administrative state made him a darling of the new right, including both Donald Trump and Benjamin Netanyahu. Tucker Carlson, during his long run at Fox News, occasionally broadcast his nightly show from Budapest, featuring fawning interviews with the big man himself. The US Conservative Political Action Conference featured Orbán at its 2022 gathering in Dallas and also at CPAC events in Budapest. Hungary, a country whose independence was twice crushed by Russia, first in 1849 and then in 1956, would, under Viktor Orbán, find greater cultural affinity with Vladimir Putin's regime than with Joe Biden's America.[15]

Concentrating power in his own hands and that of his family and friends, Orbán attacked the core of Hungary's nascent modern state and replaced it bit by bit with a bloated army of incompetent loyalists who wrecked Hungary's schools, gutted its healthcare system, and forced its most prestigious university to flee to neighboring

Austria. His brand of kleptocratic traditionalism left the country's economy in an increasingly parlous condition, and its reputation within the EU and beyond in tatters. And Hungary was not alone. In Poland, the twin brothers Lech and Jarosław Kaczyński melded Polish nationalism, conservative Catholicism, reactionary antiliberal attacks on immigrants and LGBTQ communities, and deep state conspiracy theories into a formula for near-total control of the judiciary and government agencies. After his brother Lech's death in a plane crash in Russia in 2010, Jarosław Kaczyński became Poland's de facto leader. Officially, he was merely deputy prime minister, not the prime minister or president – but everyone knew that he made all the important political decisions. And as leaked tape recordings revealed, he also seemed to have played a key role in approving or denying lucrative construction contracts in Warsaw. Kaczyński's attacks on the rule of law in Poland led the EU to block $170 billion in desperately needed pandemic recovery funds – which he explained to his supporters by saying he was really fighting a war on two fronts, against both Putin's Russia and what he called the EU "superstate." Other East-Central European EU member states, such as Slovenia, Slovakia, and the Czech Republic, were forced to contend with similar would-be patrimonial politicians in high executive positions, without thus far succumbing entirely.

Throughout the region, the matter remains far from settled. Although the Slovak electorate opted in September 2023 for a pro-Russian party, one month later Poland's voters rejected Kaczyński's patrimonial coalition led by his Law and Justice Party, a spectacular loss that handed over power to a centrist and pro-EU coalition led by Donald Tusk. Such disparate results indicate the fight continues as both sides, friends and foes of the modern state, lived to fight another day. Were the balance of power in the region to shift in favor of Russia, it is easy to imagine the assault on the modern state gaining the upper hand.[16]

* * *

The assault on the modern state has since spread well beyond Europe, but its core features have everywhere remained remarkably similar: an attack on the civil service and judiciary in the service of personalistic power. Benjamin Netanyahu's Israel is a prime example. Since 2009, whenever in office, Netanyahu worked assiduously to transfer power from state institutions to himself. In his various governments, we find the same admixture of libertarianism, religious nationalism, and executive power expansion underlying the quest to dismantle core governmental institutions throughout the West. The ultimate fate of Israel's regime type hung in the balance starting in January 2023, when Netanyahu's government proposed a series of changes to the powers of the courts that would not only undermine judicial independence, but also threaten to politicize much of the civil service. Despite weekly protests each Saturday that drew hundreds of thousands into the streets, in July 2023 the ruling coalition passed legislation removing the Supreme Court's power to turn back government decisions deemed unreasonable.

Zionism called for a refocusing of Jewish peoplehood from its religious elements to embrace political action as well. Hence the centrality of the state to modern Israel's identity. The country's founding prime minister, David Ben-Gurion, summarized the core of his political thought with the concept of *mamlakhtiut*, a term that, although derived from the Hebrew word for kingdom, is probably best translated as "stateness" (like the similar Russian and German words *gosudarstvennost'* and *Staatlichkeit*). When someone is said to have acted in a *mamlakhti* way, she is considered to be acting with the motivation of civic solidarity, in line with the interests of the state. This idea made sense in a country of newcomers from disparate ethnic and religious backgrounds. It undergirded the impressive proto-state institution building before 1948, and it justified the integration of independent militias such as the Irgun and Palmach into the Israeli army and the dismantling of educational systems linked to pre-state political parties. *Mamlakhtiut* constituted the bedrock principle of Israel's depoliticized civil service, independent courts, military, public health system, and institutions of higher education. The result was a remarkable record of modern state-building and a provision of public goods that yielded impressive growth rates, averaging 5 percent per year from 1950 to 1970 despite high defense outlays. Some critics saw in *mamlakhtiut* a collectivist orientation. On paper Ben-Gurion, after all, was a socialist. But the scholarly consensus is that Ben-Gurion remained committed to individual rights and the rule of law, at least by the standards of the day.[17]

Menachem Begin, the leader of Israel's right, did little to change this when his Likud party came to power in 1977. Although Likud is best known for its hard line on security issues, its founders placed even greater value on legality and bureaucratic rectitude than its competitors on the left. Ben-Gurion, for example, famously opposed a written constitution because he worried a society as fragmented as Israel's might descend into chaos trying to square any number of unresolvable issues. Begin insisted on the need for one, primarily to protect individual rights. He lost the argument, but both he and his party considered themselves classical liberals, institutionalists to the bone. In fact, Likud's political style – including the dress code of its leaders with their jackets and ties – remained more formal, bourgeois, and legalistic than that of Ben-Gurion's "corrupt apparatchiks." Begin also left the civil service and judiciary – staffed almost entirely during Labor Party rule – virtually untouched.[18]

As prime minister, Benjamin Netanyahu did not at first challenge this institutionialist orthodoxy. After 2009, however, he increasingly focused on himself, his power, and his household – displaying all the hallmarks of a narcissistic patrimonial strongman. With each year, Netanyahu chipped away at the state, initially on "free-market" grounds, but later primarily to benefit backers and protect his inner circle. And the assault on the state, which really picked up steam after the 2015 elections, went beyond simply shifting the balance of institutional power toward the executive. Netanyahu serially attacked the courts, the civil service, universities, and the police. Likud-led governments hectored the attorney general in the press and passed laws aimed at undermining watchdog NGOs. Likud itself focused less and less on its core principles and more on transforming itself into the "Bibi party." Backbenchers became less interested in policy, wanting little more than to fill state positions with their own clients. Supporters tarred the civil service with the American epithet "deep state," portraying them as opponents of the popular will. Observers had long noticed the "personalization" of Israeli politics, but the assault on state institutions themselves was something new.[19]

Earlier privatizations and cutbacks in state support for public institutions reflected Likud's libertarian streak, but the new attacks on state elites appealed especially to the party's base. As elsewhere, the sociology of party support in Israel breaks down much more readily along identity than along class lines. Whereas the center and left draw voters predominantly from Tel Aviv and the wealthier Ashkenazi cities of the coastal plain, Likud cultivates voters disproportionately from the Mizrahim, the roughly 50–60 percent of the Jewish population that descends from Middle Eastern rather than European origins. Many live in the poorer "development towns" of the country's peripheries. With a long history of confronting discrimination and political marginalization, they tend to be more traditional, more religious, and less educated than their Ashkenazi counterparts – and to view Israel's state bureaucracies, courts, cultural and educational institutions as staffed and led by a privileged, smug, and unelected elite. Netanyahu plays on Mizrahi resentment, despite having been the avatar of economic liberalization in Israel that sharply increased inequality. Commentators have noted the irony of their unwavering support for the scion of an elite Ashkenazi family. The left, for its part, is frequently perplexed by Mizrahi loyalty to a free-market party that works against their material interests, a discussion familiar to Americans who endlessly ponder the support for the Republican Party in poorer midwestern or southern states. As in the US, the reasons have more to do with cultural recognition than material incentives. For this community, Netanyahu had become the "good father" – *Bibi HaMelekh* (King Bibi) in the local idiom.[20]

Netanyahu's rule also illustrates a particular feature of modern patrimonialism: the reliance on inherited state capacity, even as the delegitimization and destruction of this capacity continues unabated. In 2021, early mobilization against COVID-19, as well as the rapid purchase of vaccines and subsequent vaccination of wide swaths of Israel's population, relied heavily on expert-led public health and scientific bureaucracies built up over decades, but in no way diminished Netanyahu's goal of dismantling the core bureaucratic and legal structures. In fact, rather than credit the public health service with an effective response, Netanyahu billed the purchase and distribution of the vaccine as primarily his own personal achievement. Relying on the residual expertise and capacity of the modern state, while "harvesting" it for personal benefit, has become standard practice in the modern patrimonial playbook.

Matters came to a head in 2022, when, after a brief interlude, Netanyahu returned to power in a coalition that included religious, anti-Arab, and settler partners. The religious right had long sought to transform itself from a "sector" into a hegemonic state project. Netanyahu had previously held them at bay but, facing a criminal trial for influence peddling, he needed them more than ever. What the religious nationalists, the anti-Arab parties, and the ultra-Orthodox wanted on principle, Netanyahu wanted simply to protect himself. This confluence of forces produced an unprecedented attack on the judiciary and the civil service. The Bibi party threatened to become the Bibi state.

The proposed overhaul went far beyond the earlier libertarian nostrums. Instead, the government put forward a thoroughgoing reduction of the power of the Israeli Supreme Court, the attorney general, and legal advisors within ministries, as well as the complete politicization of judicial appointments. Netanyahu sought protection from prosecution, but his allies wanted unconstrained executive power to support settlement policies that had previously been overturned by courts and administrative agencies. Equally enthusiastic were ultra-Orthodox and religious national parties, who sought to substitute Orthodox rabbinical law for civil law, to consider religious education as equivalent to secular university degrees for civil service employment, to anchor into law the sweeping exemption of all ultra-Orthodox men from military service – and to divert larger chunks of the national budget into their coffers.

Israel's institutional design renders it especially vulnerable to this sort of attack. With no written constitution, a unitary (that is, nonfederal) state structure, and a unicameral parliament, it has few checks on executive power. The Knesset can alter the fundamental rules of the political game with amendments to "basic laws" passed by a simple majority. The Supreme Court, which since 1992 has gathered increased powers to review governmental acts, has become virtually the only check on executive and ministerial authority. In addition, the country's attorney general retained powers independent from the prime minister, while legal advisors within ministries reporting to the attorney general could issue binding rulings on the legality of ministerial decisions.

The judicial overhaul – or "judicial coup," in the parlance of those who demonstrated against it after its details were revealed in January 2023 – amounted to a sprawling set of amendments to the country's basic laws designed to shift power in favor of the Knesset and, ultimately, the prime minister. The blueprint had been published years earlier in a series of policy papers of the Kohelet Policy Forum, a small Israeli think-tank funded by American billionaires. Its motto: "national sovereignty and individual liberty." The authors of these papers argue for small government libertarianism, religious nationalism, and enhanced power for the Knesset over judges and state officials. In all these respects, the Kohelet Policy Forum closely tracks the agenda of the Federalist Society and other conservative organizations in the United States. Most Israelis are familiar with American culture, but the adoption of the Kohelet papers into the language of the law represented a wholesale import of something foreign to Israeli political life.

In the January 2023 proposal, the body selecting judges, the Judicial Selection Board, would now include an absolute majority of politicians (and among them a majority of ruling coalition members) alongside representatives appointed by the coalition and a small minority of judges. The scope of reviewable administrative acts and legislation would be diminished, and the Knesset could in any case override many rulings with a simple majority vote. The independence and power of the attorney general would be reduced, and legal advisors to government ministries would be reclassified from independent officials reporting to the justice ministry to political appointees whose rulings would be advisory rather than binding. Beyond the judicial overhaul, the ruling coalition began eyeing state bureaucracies and the country's universities for partisan takeover and/or demolition.

Netanyahu's allies saw dark conspiracies behind the hundreds of thousands of protesters who week after week flooded the streets in loud and raucous demonstrations. As noted by one official: "We are following what is happening. This is a very high-level organization. There is an organized center from which all the demonstrators branch out in an orderly manner ... Who finances the transportation, the flags, the stages? It's clear to us." Netanyahu's son, Yair, led the Twitter charge against the protests, accusing Europeans, Arabs, and even the American deep state of secretly pulling the strings. The US Department of State and the White House issued a sharp rebuke and denied any meddling. A shouting match ensued at the Netanyahu residence, where Yair, then thirty years old, still lived with his parents. Bibi and his wife Sara – who, like Yair, was unelected yet politically influential – told their son that he had gone too far. Yair had to shutter his Twitter account before going into temporarily exile in New York and then Puerto Rico, where he was guarded by minders from the Israel Security Agency while hanging out with a crypto billionaire.[21]

In the face of the increasingly disruptive demonstrations, rising refusals of Israeli citizens to report for military reserve duty, and intensified criticism from the United States and the Jewish diaspora, Netanyahu at first put a pause on the legislative process in an attempt to dial down the temperature. By summer 2023, however, the first basic law amendment had passed, reducing the Supreme Court's scope for rejecting government acts. In its entirety, however, the overhaul lost credibility. Many Likud voters claimed not to have voted for such revolutionary changes, and some Likud Knesset members announced their intention to oppose further institutional erosion without broader social consensus. Netanyahu's government, however, depended upon the support of the judicial coup's most ardent proponents, the religious, anti-Arab, and settler parties.

The opposition immediately appealed the amendment to the Basic Law to the Supreme Court, setting up a constitutional showdown. Could the court in effect declare a constitutional amendment that guts the power of the judiciary unconstitutional? The stakes were high not only for democracy, but also for the broader question of whether Israel's state would begin to resemble many of its Arab neighbors – inefficient, ineffective, and corrupt.

Such a prospect seemed increasingly likely as the civil service continued to suffer relentless attacks by Netanyahu and his loyalists. Several high-level officials, including a number of the director generals in charge of day-to-day management of Israeli state agencies, gave up and left. The director general of the education ministry, Asaf Zalel, explained in his letter of resignation: "The rift we have reached [in society] does not allow me to continue to fulfill my responsibilities as required." The public diplomacy minister, Galit Distel Atbaryan, fired her own director general after widespread media reports of the minister's abusive behavior; it turned out that the senior bureaucrat had most likely quit. When Miri Regev, Likud transportation minister, tried to appoint her own former aide to the post of director general, the Public Service Senior Appointments Advisory Committee rejected him as unqualified. She appointed him anyway as "stand-in deputy director general" for six months before ramming the candidacy through, claiming that he had now gained the necessary experience. In other ministries, rather than risk rejection of incompetent cronies, Netanyahu's ministers chose to leave director general positions vacant. Cronyism is always a bug of public administration, but under Netanyahu it had become a feature. "They don't even try to hide it," said one dejected civil servant interviewed by the left liberal daily *Haaretz*. In her summary of the situation, Hebrew University political scientist Gayil Talshir put it succinctly: "What Netanyahu wants is personal loyalty, not professionalism." Demoralization among those who remained was widespread as management fell into the hands of hacks and incompetents.[22]

The bill for a cowed bureaucracy and diminished expertise came due on October 7, 2023, when Hamas operatives from Gaza carried out the largest single-day slaughter of Jewish civilians since the Holocaust. Having ignored multiple intelligence warnings of an impending attack, the Netanyahu government left the towns and kibbutzim bordering Gaza defenseless. The tragedy was compounded in the days that followed by a shockingly feeble state that scrambled to respond with public resources to assist survivors, treat the injured, identify and bury the dead, repair damaged and burned homes, and prepare a military counterattack. Four days after the Hamas attack, one source with access to senior government officials reported: "There are entire systems that don't function because of the appointment of Likud people and those close to the government, which don't function because they don't have any relevant abilities. This includes the senior echelon in the ministries of welfare, transportation, education and even the treasury, which is partially paralyzed due to a personal quarrel between the chief accountant and the budget department. The only ministry that functions is the ministry of health, thanks to the director general and a relatively reasonable minister."

For the first week after the Hamas terrorist invasion, Israel's civil society rather than its paralyzed state led the way. Army units reported shortages of supplies of almost every sort, from ceramic vests to fresh food. Parents of soldiers and civil society organizations stepped into the breach. Brothers in Arms, a group of soldiers involved in the protest against the judicial reform (and tarred as traitors by governing coalition politicians), in no time organized a command post to send food and supplies to military units. Parallel to this effort, the women's NGO Building an Alternative, which had also mobilized originally to oppose the judicial reform while dressed in their signature "Handmaid's Tale" red robes, repurposed its national organization to resupply Israeli defense and intelligence units. As time went on, the Israeli Defense Forces and the domestic security service regained its footing, but in the initial week, the state remained largely a no-show. The tragic breakdown of Israel's security directly reflected a state weakened by almost a decade of patrimonial politics.

* * *

The gravest challenge and most shocking development of all has been the personalization of state authority in the erstwhile heartlands of the rule of law itself – the United Kingdom and the United States. The admixture of grievances generating personalistic rule in these two countries differed in meaningful ways, but they were similar enough to seal an alliance between Boris Johnson and Donald Trump.

Boris Johnson became prime minister in 2019 with a singled-minded determination to distance his country from "Brussels bureaucrats," whom he has explicitly labeled representatives of the deep state. His staunch commitment to Brexit also informed his turn against the civil service, which was widely believed to be hostile to his anti-EU agenda. His general disregard for following legal rules, along with cabinet appointments based more on personal loyalty than competence, not only inhibited crucial coordination with European public health officials during the COVID-19 pandemic, but also sent his country's economy into a tailspin. At the height of the pandemic, Johnson and his appointee pals continually and ostentatiously flouted strict rules on assembly. While the citizenry could not attend funerals or sit at hospital bedsides, Johnson was having Christmas parties with his mates at 10 Downing Street. People couldn't leave their homes – but Johnson's spin-doctor, Dominic Cummings, went for a 260-mile drive to Barnard Castle, claiming it was for an "eye test."[23]

Morale among British civil servants plummeted as they were vilified and bullied by Johnson's ministers. The result was a significant weakening of British state capacity that continues to pose severe challenges to Johnson's successors. Yet even while wrecking the British state, Johnson managed to reward his major benefactors, adding fully eighty-six of his friends and associates to the House of Lords – including twenty-seven donors to the Conservative Party, the son of a former KGB agent who had hosted him on weekend trips to Umbria, and his own brother Jo Johnson, now formally ennobled as Baron Johnson of Marylebone.[24]

Russia clearly had an interest in weakening Europe, and Brexit was a logical vehicle. A well-funded Russian influence operation played a role in the success of the Brexit campaign, in which a deeply divided society voted 52 percent to leave the EU and 48 to remain. The city's "laundromat," through which Russian oligarchs washed their money, gave Putin a built-in lobby. The authors of the "Russia Report" by the UK's Parliamentary Intelligence and Security Committee noted that the country's intelligence and security services "underestimated the response required to the Russian threat and are still playing catch up." Although the report maintains that Russia played no direct role in the voting process, it left open the possibility that Kremlin-sponsored information efforts, especially through the state-funded Sputnik press agency and the RT television channel, may have helped to tip the scales. In such a closely fought referendum, if one in fifty voters had changed their vote, the results would have been different.[25]

But the roots of Brexit ran much deeper than the Russian influence campaign. A strong undercurrent of anti-EU sentiment had been a staple of the British press since the UK joined in 1973. Boris Johnson himself, during his stint as the *Telegraph*'s reporter in Brussels beginning in 1989, emerged as relentless critic of the European Commission. His articles told tales of Brussels hiring sniffers to ensure uniformity of the smell of European manure. He invoked the old half-truth of the Commission controlling the curvature of bananas, while inventing new ones, such as the standardization of condom sizes. Behind these clownish assertions, however, lay a common thread of distaste for the regulatory state (or "nanny state" he termed it, in typical libertarian parlance), based on worries about diminished national sovereignty and fears of a less English England. Boris was a clown, and a pompous clown at that. But the cultural zeitgeist rewarded this unapologetic avatar of Anglican, Etonian, and Oxbridge English traditionalism – a middle-class version of Churchill, with no respect or patience for pettifogging European legalism.[26]

The geography of the Leave vote revealed something more serious, however. It aligned neatly with regions of economic distress, declining middle-class incomes, older white voters, and popular concern over immigration and cultural heterogeneity, all of which had picked up steam since the financial meltdown in 2008. The Leave campaign took advantage of these fissures in British society. Much of its strategy entailed spreading falsehoods or distortions that tapped into the vague insecurities of older, middle- and working-class, and white voters: that the European Commission issues legislation (it doesn't); that 60 percent of UK laws derived from EU law (also untrue); that plans were afoot to create a European army that would replace Britain's (an invention); that Turkey was preparing to join the EU (it wasn't close and, in any case, this would for many member states trigger a further referendum); that the EU had plans to dismantle the National Health System (no EU member state would consider such a move); and that European integration had led to illegal immigration. All of these points – especially the last one – were deployed to create a climate of fear.

Promises were issued by the Leave campaign that could not possibly be kept, the most notorious ones being a supposed £350 million per week in British payments to the EU that would magically fill the coffers of the NHS after a vote to "leave"; the claim that UK nationals living in EU member states would be unaffected by Brexit; and the promise that severed European trade ties would be replaced by a closer relationship with Donald Trump's America. Objective and modestly stated reports from experts within the civil service and academia outlining the costs of leaving the EU, and the consequences for Brits living abroad, were smeared as bought and paid-for EU propaganda. As if all this were not enough, "Remain" waged a baleful campaign. The virtues of staying in "Europe" were regarded as self-evident, divisions within and between pro-EU Tories and Labour forestalled a unified message, and hardly anyone offered a full-throated defense of the EU to counter the transgressive energy of the Leave campaign. Remain was a no-show, and it lost.

Having narrowly prevailed in the referendum, Brexiteers had no concrete plan for actual exit. Endless and frustrating negotiations dragged on, generating humorous memes on social media, such as photos of futuristic spacecraft moving through the galaxy with the caption: "The year is 2297 and humans have moved into outer space, but the final Brexit agreement has yet to be negotiated." The thorniest issue concerned the status of Northern Ireland, which stood to lose its tariff-free customs union with the Republic of Ireland in a "hard Brexit" unless a side deal could be reached. The Northern Ireland Protocol, ratified in January 2020, managed to split the difference but remained highly imperfect, ultimately leading to a "border" of sorts between Britain and Northern Ireland with customs checks and paperwork. Not only did this threaten Northern Ireland's economy, but it also brought into question the 1998 Good Friday Agreement that brought an end to the violent conflict in the region by ensuring its ties to Great Britain.

The Northern Ireland Protocol directly contradicted explicit promises Johnson had made to the British public. He had declared in December 2019: "There will be no checks on goods going from Great Britain to Northern Ireland, or Northern Ireland to Great Britain." He proclaimed in August 2020 (and several times thereafter): "There will be no border down the Irish Sea ... over my dead body." In effect, Johnson thought of Northern Ireland as traditional English "patrimony" rather than as a legally constituted subunit within the UK, with legal relationships that needed to be carefully worked out. Defining borders historically and not legally is a key part of the patrimonial playbook, a feature of his thinking that Johnson apparently shares with Putin concerning the status of Crimea and "Novorossiya," with Benjamin Netanyahu concerning the West Bank, and with Viktor Orbán concerning lands "lost" to Hungary after World War I in Slovakia, Romania, Ukraine, and Serbia. It was perhaps unsurprising, then, that Orbán was the second EU leader to visit Johnson at 10 Downing Street after the completion of Brexit, following only the Irish Prime Minister who had met with Johnson to ratify the Northern Ireland Protocol.[27]

Johnson's arbitrary, narcissistic leadership style also wreaked havoc on the British response to the COVID-19 pandemic. Flagrantly violating his own government's lockdown policies, Johnson and his cronies secretly partied, maskless and at close quarters, while millions of British citizens faced death and debilitating illness. Leaked videos of these gatherings generated widespread public outrage, followed by prolonged parliamentary inquiries that finally undermined the prime minister's political legitimacy. His chaotic and scandal-plagued premiership came to an end in July 2022.

Yet the unholy alliance of libertarianism, cultural traditionalism, and executive arbitrariness that had done so much damage to the British state under Johnson's leadership did not suddenly disappear. He was succeeded by Liz Truss, who had been his last foreign secretary and had led the negotiations on the Northern Ireland Protocol. In her campaign for the party leadership, Truss called for an attack on the "woke" civil service, dubbing it the "war on Whitehall." Confronting the inflationary fallout from COVID and Brexit, Truss directly followed the bad advice of hard-core libertarian think-tanks, simultaneously ending subsidized energy prices for households and businesses while initiating broad tax cuts and large governmental borrowing. Financial instability quickly ensued, followed by hefty criticism, a policy reversal, and the collapse of the Tory government, making Truss the shortest-serving prime minister in British history. Her replacement, Rishi Sunak, struggled to define a winning governing formula that built on what the Conservative Party had become. Like Truss, he confronted a paradox: Brexit may have liberated the UK from Brussels, but the state itself remained deeply embedded in British society, its functions indispensable, and its programs mostly popular. The Tories had long attacked the "blob," a term that had come to encompass virtually every ministry of government and its civil servants, judges, lawyers critical of conservatives, judicial review, the media, universities, regulators, and pretty much the entire cultural left – in short, what the American and European right now term the "woke" establishment. Of course, none of this amounted to a program for governing, but few Tory stalwarts seemed interested in the machinery of government and the details of public policy. The *Financial Times* characterized the new plan as an attack on "Big Everything": "Big State, Big Media, Big Quango, Big Finance, Big Judiciary, Big Green – big anything else you don't like."[28]

* * *

The United States is the most shocking case of all. The coronavirus highlighted an American state, so formidable on the global stage with its capacity to project unparalleled military force, as incapable of fulfilling crucial public health functions. The national public health bureaucracy, as it evolved under President Donald Trump, was overwhelmed and quickly found itself unable to manage the country's newfound status in spring 2020 as the global epicenter of the coronavirus pandemic.

The problem was partly due to American federalism, in which the states are left to perform so many public health tasks. But it was more than that. Crucial bureaucracies went unstaffed in the Trump administration, with agency heads unconfirmed by the Senate. That was by design rather than by default. Trump preferred it that way because it fostered personal dependence. "I like 'acting'," he noted in 2019 when asked about having so many "acting" cabinet secretaries. "It gives me more flexibility."[29]

All presidents grapple with the trade-off between expertise and political loyalty in staffing senior positions, but in the Trump administration personal loyalty took precedence over professional qualifications or adherence to shared ideals. The American state had been assembled gradually over decades to deal with an increasingly large and complex society. But Trump's presidency meant a major step backward from the perspective of administrative competence. During the presidential election campaign Trump promised to staff his administration with the "best people," but once in power this vision devolved into a preference for family, friends, and sycophants. Executive power under Trump was managed more like a king's (chaotic) court than a normal presidential administration. Rather than maintain a sharp distinction between his private interests and the public interest, Trump deliberately blurred the lines between them.

As in the cases of Orbán and Johnson, Trump's disdain for the civil service was apparent from the very outset of his administration. At times he seemed intent on choosing department secretaries who disliked their unit's mission or even its very existence: Andrew Puzder at the department of labor, Rick Perry as secretary of energy, and Betsy DeVos in the department of education are the most prominent examples. From the first days of the administration, political appointees regarded as unqualified were deployed to purge the bureaucracy. Senior civil servants with expertise in food security, climate science, HIV/AIDS prevention, and childhood nutrition were sidelined, consistently ignored, or shown the door. Although the broad exodus of career officials from the Department of State received much attention, the elimination of a small team in the White House focusing specifically on pandemic preparedness did not – that is, until the spring of 2020.[30]

Trump distrusted anyone who might diminish his personal power and authority. He called on experts to pitch in when needed – especially when he became ill himself with the virus in October 2020 – only to shunt them aside when they contradicted or outshined him. When upstaged by Dr. Anthony Fauci and the much-diminished public health bureaucracy he represented at the daily White House coronavirus briefing, Trump repeatedly sidelined experts until he hit on those less likely to appear to challenge his wisdom and instincts. Rather than give over responsibility for the US COVID-19 response to the appropriate federal health agencies, Trump chose to attack the experts and declare that the deep state had blocked what he claimed were cheap and easy cures, ranging from hydroxychloroquine and ivermectin to exposure to ultraviolet light. The horrified look on White House coronavirus response coordinator Deborah Birx's face when the president seemed to be advising millions of frightened Americans to inject themselves with "disinfectant" encapsulates the danger posed by the assault on the modern state. "I didn't know how to handle that episode," Birx later said, "I still think about it every day."[31]

The COVID crisis did not just challenge the Trump presidency; it destroyed it. But it did not have to be that way. Everyone understood that dealing with a once-in-a-century global pandemic wasn't going to be easy. If Trump had leveled with American people, if he had shown even a modicum of empathy for the suffering and anxiety of others, and, most crucially, if he had handed the entire matter over to those who actually knew something, the experts within the public health bureaucracy and the universities, he could have emerged as a hero. But Trump's assault on the state and its expert officials, and the resulting chaos and death toll, generated just enough craving for normality that it may have cost Trump an election he otherwise had a chance of winning. That's the political toll. Tallying the human toll is more difficult. One method is comparison: if the US had Canada's death rate from COVID, 350,000 Americans would still be alive. In congressional testimony, Dr. Birx put the numbers of needless deaths at closer to half a million.[32]

We dwell upon Trump's COVID response not only because it was emblematic of his presidency, but because it highlights the risks posed by patrimonial rulers when confronted with the complex challenges of modern government. Like Putin, Orbán, and Netanyahu, Trump combined his attacks on the modern state with efforts to promote the interests of members of his extended household. During his entire presidency, Trump's sons Donald Jr. and Eric continued to manage the Trump Organization on their father's behalf, blurring the lines between the state and the Trump family business. Trump himself refused to put his assets in a blind trust or even to reveal his past income taxes. His daughter Ivanka accompanied her father to important diplomatic meetings, such as the 2019 G-20 gathering in Osaka, Japan, where she squeezed herself awkwardly into official photos and conversations with world leaders such as Japanese Prime Minister Shinzo Abe, French President Emmanuel Macron, and IMF Director Christine Lagarde. As US Ambassador to South Korea Christopher Hill aptly explained: "It looks to the rest of the world like we have a kind of a constitutional monarchy ... It's increasingly problematic in terms of our credibility ... It says to our allies, to everyone we do business with, that the only people who matter are Trump and his family members." Meanwhile, Ivanka's husband Jared Kushner combined his job spearheading the procurement of medical equipment to fight the pandemic – Project Airbridge – with a high-profile diplomatic role as senior advisor to the president on Middle East affairs. The latter gave him the opportunity to engage in personal outreach to the ruling families of Saudi Arabia, Qatar, and the United Arab Emirates, which later invested billions of dollars in Kushner's private investment firm.[33]

Trump's approach in his first term in office might seem to have reflected inexperience rather than principle, but his campaign materials and speeches in the 2024 campaign indicated otherwise. Building on his particularly toxic brew of libertarianism, Christian nationalism, and especially his faith in unrestricted presidential power, he took aim on his campaign website at the independence of virtually every congressionally mandated agency of the federal government, vowing to subordinate them to presidential authority. "What we are trying to do is identify the pockets of independence and seize them," declared Trump's former director of office of management and budget. Trump vowed to impound, rather than spend, funds appropriated by Congress for regulatory agencies that did not meet his approval. And regardless of promises made by Trump before his first presidential term to hire "the best people," his former personnel chief had learned from the "mistake" of Trump's own appointees limiting his personal power: "It's not enough to get the personnel right. What's necessary is a complete system overhaul."[34]

In essence, Trump promised to rejoin the battle against the civil service. As already noted at the start of this book,

Trump's aides crafted an executive order at the end of his first term, "Creating Schedule F in the Excepted Service," which curtailed employment protections from a crucial group of career officials – an order Trump signed but Biden reversed. During the 2024 campaign, Trump declared in his characteristic style his intention to reinstate the order if re-elected. In March 2023, at a rally in Waco, he warned: "Either the deep state destroys America or we destroy the deep state." In June he continued this train of reasoning: "We will demolish the deep state ... We will expel the warmongers from our government. We will drive out the globalists. We will cast out the communists, Marxists, and fascists ... And we will throw off the sick political class that hates our country."[35]

By the end of the Trump presidency, the assault on the administrative state, although facing stiff resistance in some quarters, had left in its wake colossal damage. The administration of President Joe Biden, upon taking office, worked diligently to restore bureaucratic oversight in key areas of environmental, health, and foreign policy. But Trump and his competitors for the Republican nomination for the 2024 presidential election remained united in their vilification of the "deep state." As Florida Governor Ron DeSantis's own challenge to Donald Trump floundered in summer 2023, he announced a change of direction in a memo to supporters: "More to come in the Fall of 2023 ... including woke military, the deep state, school choice and beyond." In addition to Trump's "MAGA" think-tanks, more mainstream ones had their own plans for a renewed assault on the state, including the Heritage Foundation, a think-tank that has helped selected personnel and design policies of Republican administrations since the Reagan presidency. With the three Trump-appointed Supreme Court justices joining a majority seemingly committed to eliminating longstanding traditions of deference to federal agencies, the fate of the American administrative state remains highly uncertain.[36]

* * *

Close observers of politics have long noted the diffusion of particularly successful regime types from country to country – whether for good or for ill. Whether it's due to geopolitical influence, active imitation, or simply something in the air – the zeitgeist – what happens in one society affects another. On the positive side, the ideals of liberal democracy articulated in the American and French revolutions of the eighteenth century, despite all their hypocrisies and imperfections, have generated repeated waves of democratization in every region of the globe. The remarkable combination of inclusive electoral institutions and well-governed legal states, where it has been consolidated, has repeatedly shown an ability to generate stable and peaceful political order, dynamic economic growth, and generous welfare state protections. It's no wonder that the liberal democratic regime type has been so widely emulated. Unfortunately, bad regime types also seem to spread in a wave-like manner. In the twentieth century, the emulation of fascism and communism in the wake of the Great Depression led to mass violence and political repression in countries around the world.

The diffusion of personalistic, patrimonial rule in Russia and Eurasia, East-Central Europe, and now the core liberal democratic countries of the West in the twenty-first century thus fits with earlier historical patterns of regime change in response to social crisis. Unfortunately, the global patrimonial wave also tends to reinforce the autocratic power of patrimonial leaders in middle- and low-income countries. Leaders like Erdoğan in Turkey, Modi in India, or Bolsonaro in Brazil, whose own patrimonial regimes trampled on human rights and the rule of law, used to be shunned and criticized by the international community. Now, they forge alliances with their patrimonial colleagues in Russia, Europe, and North America, proudly collaborating to complete the task of undermining the global liberal order. If they succeed, the result will not only be the end of the long historical era of liberal democratic global dominance, but will also introduce the very real possibility that the experiment of modern statecraft itself will come to a crashing end. The consequences for public health, safety, and prosperity – especially in the middle of a terrifying global climate crisis that cannot be tackled successfully without expert advice, strong and sustained international cooperation, and the strict enforcement of carefully designed legal regulations to limit carbon emissions – can scarcely be imagined.

6

Reclaiming the Modern State

The apparatus of the modern state is big, generally dependable, and yet mostly invisible. Deeply valued state programs like Medicare and Social Security have become so enmeshed in American society that voters sometimes forget they are even part of the "state" they have learned to hate so much. The state gets noticed mostly in two situations – either when state bureaucrats make terrible mistakes, or when we want the state to help us, but it is too weak to do so.

In the first case, state malfeasance – or mismanagement – that gains wide press coverage only appears to confirm people's worst fears about "unelected bureaucrats," even when such bad outcomes are quite atypical. As Michael Lewis has pointed out, the Obama administration's decision to provide $535 million in start-up funding for the failed solar energy company Solyndra, for example, garnered multiple headlines and inspired countless scathing editorials, while successful government loans to hundreds of other alternative energy companies in the same program were scarcely mentioned. The fate of most state officials in the modern era is to toil for moderate wages in obscurity

– yet more frequently than most people realize, these officials are the source of policies and innovations that have vastly improved the quality of our lives in comparison to premodern times.[1]

We also notice the state when we find ourselves in deep crises that cry out for an effective government response. This is probably why, in spring 2020, as tens of thousands died per day in the first months of the COVID-19 pandemic, a remarkable thing happened. In cities large and small across the nation and around the world – in New York, Florida, and California; in Ireland, Italy, Spain, and Turkey – people lined up on streets and balconies, stopped their cars, or opened their apartment windows yelling their thanks, clapping in recognition of the work performed by thousands of public service workers and first responders. Frightened, confused publics thus turned to the state in their hour of need. People wanted information, solace, and reassurance. Instead, in countries run by patrimonial leaders, they frequently got buffoonery, cynicism, and the denigration of government experts. Even as the pandemic faded and the death count fell, instead of recognizing the dedicated staff of our public health agencies for the heroes they are, Ron DeSantis chose to criticize his rival Donald Trump for "turning the country over to Fauci in March 2020."[2]

As horrific as COVID-19 was, in a way we got lucky. Without the expertise of established government health agencies, many more could have perished. The production of an effective COVID vaccine through "Operation Warp Speed" was an unusual example of a highly successful Trump-era state program that relied on the expertise of professional scientists and health professionals who were given great autonomy in their work – even if Trump later hesitated to take credit for it, given the antivaccine sentiments of so many of his supporters. Without the expertise of well-trained central bankers – who, to their credit, had learned some important lessons from their mistakes after the 2008 financial crisis – the economic damage also might have been even worse. What will come next? What will be the next collective challenge? Sometimes we need to build or do big things together as a society. The modern administrative state is the best vehicle humans have yet devised for doing just that. Part of investing in and valuing the state involves hedging against the risk of low probability, but high-cost, events like a once-in-a-century pandemic. But perhaps just as crucially, our quotidian existence seems, well, quotidian because of the secure governance framework constituted by many thousands of small administrative acts. And it is remarkable how quickly our collective existence begins to fray – whether through the disintegration of transportation networks, the failure of electric grids, or the collapse of public order itself – when the state and its regulatory agencies are no longer there.

The assault on the state and the spread of patrimonial rule to every part of the planet since the early years of this century has already done a great deal of damage. The accompanying shift from the rule of law to the rule of men has diminished our quality of life. The attack on the modern state by patrimonial and would-be patrimonial leaders did not just undermine public health agencies around the world as humanity confronted the devastating COVID-19 pandemic, resulting in untold additional death and suffering. It has also inhibited the regulation of huge and potentially unstable markets, such as those for financial instruments like cryptocurrency exchanges and credit default swaps, which render us vulnerable to a repeat of the 2008 meltdown. It has delayed or derailed our collective response to climate change during what may well be our final chance to prevent the most catastrophic outcomes of global warming. And it has eroded public confidence and trust in state agencies across the board – including those tasked with regulating elections and tabulating their results, with ominous implications for the future of competitive democracy. In sum, global organized efforts to dismantle the modern state have been remarkably successful. No one is happy with the results, with sizeable majorities in the United States and elsewhere saying that their countries are "on the wrong track." Yet as the performance of state agencies declines under the pressure of these relentless attacks, its opponents continue to call for even greater cutbacks in state funding, hiring, and regulatory oversight.

Depicting this wave as primarily a "populist" attack on democracy constitutes a misdiagnosis – or at least an underestimation of the pathology – and points us potentially to the wrong cure. As important as defending democracy is, and as grave as the danger posed by a Putin or a Trump, the rot introduced by their personalistic rule is systemic and will endure long past the point when both have left the scene. New elections alone cannot reverse state decay. Not only has doubt been cast on the impartiality and expertise of our public administration, but this attack on meritocratic government comes at a time when the existing US federal workforce is rapidly aging. The number of federal employees over the age of sixty has increased from 162,000 in 2006 to more than 325,000 in 2022. Only around 7 percent are under the age of thirty.[3]

Fortunately, there is a path forward. The assault on the modern state, supported by libertarian conservatives, religious nationalists, and advocates of unitary executive theory, and transformed in a profoundly destructive way by this new wave of leaders, can be effectively countered by a renewed appreciation for the modern state – for the civil servants, impartial judiciaries, and professional experts that make both democracy and prosperity possible in a complex, interdependent world. When those leading the attack speak of the deep state, they simply mean the state itself, and that is what must be confronted directly.

Some readers at this stage may conclude that we are romanticizing the state and its workforce. After all, state bureaucrats *do* sometimes try to impose misguided regulations in ways that genuinely hamper the economy and interfere with individual liberty. Are we ignoring the dark side of the modern state here? To this charge we believe there are two responses. First, in response to those who always prefer the "efficiency of the market" to "government tyranny," we suggest spending some time deciphering or challenging a bank statement, returning a defective car or computer to the manufacturer, or simply chasing down lost luggage with an airline. In disputes like this, service within the public sector is sometimes faster, more polite, and more sincere than what one receives from the "call center" – if one can even reach a real person at the customer service number instead of a convoluted phone tree or an AI-generated algorithm. After decades of laughing at and denigrating "state workers," perhaps the time has come to point the finger in the other direction.

Second, we are happy to concede that there are times when criticism of particular state bureaucracies can be right on target. We defend the modern state not because we love lazy bureaucrats or somehow want the world to be run like the department of motor vehicles. Both of us were trained as Sovietologists, becoming specialists on lethargic state enterprises making shoddy goods that no one really wanted. We have a deep appreciation for the pathologies of centrally planned economies. Too much state can be bad. But we urgently need to regain an appreciation for just how ugly the alternatives to the impersonal modern state truly are.

The crucial difference between the modern state and its patrimonial alternatives is sometimes obscured by the presence not only of powerful political families but also of occasional outright corruption within Western democracies. The Kennedys and Bushes in the United States and the Trudeaus in Canada remind us of the continuing power and allure of family dynasties in modern politics. The sons and daughters of these political families may be competent and their commitment to public service sincere, but the potential for translating public power into private wealth, for treating the state as a family business – as the suspicion over Hunter Biden's access to his father shows – does not somehow magically disappear.

What, then, is the difference between patrimonial and nonpatrimonial rulers in the modern world? Our choice is not between patrimonialism and perfect legal proceduralism. No such purity exists in politics. The choice instead is between the lure of family bonds within legal constraints – or without them. The difference is crucial, for those who attempt to reconstruct political legitimacy along patrimonial lines will always seek to discredit the modern state entirely, rather than defend themselves within its rules. And once the legal framework of the modern state is eviscerated, rulers and their "extended households" can grab the state's assets and redistribute them to loyalists with nearly complete impunity.

In this respect, at least, a good state *is* a deep state – not in the sense of having hidden unaccountable power, but in the sense of being embedded in our culture, in our educational institutions, and in our broader societies as a profoundly necessary part of our world. The contemporary appeal of rule by the "good father" reflects deeply held longings for traditional community in a time of rapid dislocation, as well as the economic interests of those left behind by globalization. Yet history has shown that cherished local communities are better preserved, defended, and supported under modern state institutions than under the archaic personalistic forms of a bygone era.

* * *

What then should be done? Notwithstanding all the troubling trends we have recounted in this book, it is not too late to reverse the tide. The battle to save the modern state will not be easy. It will require sustained collective action by those of us who still appreciate the relative safety, security, and prosperity of modern life, against what is sure to be concerted opposition by powerful politicians and well-funded interest groups who benefit directly from the dismantling of legal constraints and public agencies. Yet if the analysis we have presented in this book is correct, nothing less than our human future is at stake.

To combat the patrimonial wave and restore the modern state, four steps above all are vitally necessary. First, we must diagnose the problem clearly and educate the public about what lies ahead if the modern state is dismantled. Second, we need to resist both leftwing and communitarian Utopian schemes for replacing the liberal state; instead, we should double down on the defense of our existing state apparatus against its enemies. Third, we must mobilize public sentiment in support of the hardworking people who staff state agencies in countries around the world, issuing a global call to public service that might entice our best young minds to devote themselves to careers in government. Fourth, we need to reorient our foreign policy to include the defense of rule-of-law states – and not just democracy – as a top priority. We now know that the assault on the modern state is a worldwide phenomenon, and our collective response has to be an international one.

Let's begin with the problem of diagnosis. What should we be looking for? What are the key indicators of impending patrimonialism? In order to assess the degree to which the rule of men is replacing the modern legal state, it's important that we identify the primary steps in the process of establishing patrimonial rule. Three features, in particular, stand out in this regard: the increasing promotion of family members and cronies to positions of power, concerted attacks on legally constituted state agencies and those who work for them, and the delegitimization of expert knowledge as a qualification for government positions.

Rule by the leader's extended household. In many ways, this is the core of patrimonial rule: the creation of a state that functions as a "family business" of sorts. In the modern world, this entails building up the household as an alternative to normal sites of governmental function. Family members of the ruler and/or his cronies increasingly muscle their way into positions of power, appearing on behalf of the leader regardless of their formal qualifications. Instead of preserving a strict separation between government offices and private residences, the patrimonial leader recreates a kind of royal "court" that those personally loyal to the leader periodically visit to attend meals, celebrations, and even discussions of state policy.

The attack on the civil service, the judiciary, and government agencies. As political power is increasingly concentrated in the executive, the system of civil service, with employees hired, promoted, and compensated according to impartial legal rules, is replaced with the doling out of state positions to those who have personal connections to the patrimonial leader's extended "household." Nonpartisan judges and prosecutors evaluated for their legal expertise are replaced with partisans who must demonstrate their personal loyalty in high-profile court cases to keep their jobs. The concept of state agencies as providers of the public good is replaced with conspiracy theories about "unelected bureaucrats" who wield power on behalf of the "deep state."

Elimination of professional expertise as a criterion for government positions. The idea that only those with sufficient training and education should be granted sufficient autonomy to implement policy in their areas of expertise is anathema to patrimonial politics, which is built on the arbitrary power of the ruler in all spheres of policy. Accordingly, patrimonial leaders do their best to undermine the independent power of professional experts in politics in every sphere. They publicly ridicule scientists whose advice contradicts the whims of the ruler. They seek to subordinate institutions of higher education that try to maintain their autonomy to hire faculty, design the curriculum, and grant advanced degrees, setting up alternative educational organizations more loyal to the leader. And they trumpet the "common sense" of ordinary people – as interpreted by the patrimonial ruler – as a surer guide to public policy than the carefully deliberated professional opinions of experts.[4]

Taken together, these three indicators of patrimonialism amount to the replacement of rule of law with rule of men. This is the core task of would-be patrimonial leaders: the reconstruction of the basis of political legitimacy itself. And this task has been accomplished with partial to complete success now in countries around the world – in both democracies and in authoritarian regimes, in rich societies and in poorer ones, and in polities on every continent.

* * *

Fortunately, there appears to be an appetite for reversing the tide and for a renewed honoring of careers of public service. But building a new consensus in support of the modern state will require not only defeating the assault from the right but also addressing some of the most cherished arguments of the progressive left, focusing, not unexpectedly, on the promotion of popular participation and social justice. These critics begin with the observation that bureaucracy is frequently unaccountable, with the potential for disregarding the viewpoints of the most marginalized sectors of society. Their preferred solutions to this problem carry different labels – "permanent democracy," "governance-driven democratization," and "recursive democratization" are representative slogans – but all focus on radically increasing the participation of citizens in day-to-day administrative decision-making. Some of the proposals, such as more citizen consultation, seem benign and are already practiced. Expanding them would most likely do no harm. Others, however, go far beyond this. "While elections have long had a pride of place in democratic theory," K. Sabeel Rahman notes, "thickening our democratic capacities and experience requires that we turn instead to front-line institutions of governance, such as regulatory agencies." The administrative state itself, in this line of thought, should become an arena of democracy.[5]

These and similar contemporary proposals have a long pedigree, stretching back to the Paris Commune and running through early soviet (the Russian word for "council") democracy that emerged in the chaotic wake of World War I in Russia and Germany. Notwithstanding the good intentions behind them, however, the modern versions suffer from the same weaknesses as the classical variants. Advocates of direct citizen engagement in administrative decision-making present no plausible institutional design by which this could happen with sufficient alacrity and resolution to be practical. Instead, like the earlier experiments in radically participatory democracy, these new proposals would likely be recipes for inefficiency and chaos – the very sort of social environment that facilitates calls for a return of the "good father." What the patrimonial right wants, the radical democratic left might accidentally provide through its own misplaced idealism. The best way to reclaim the state is to situate it properly within a liberal democratic society rather than risk dissolving it in a failed experiment.

Others of a more communitarian bent see the major problem of the modern West today as the stultifying rule of the college-educated "meritocracy." Theorists like Daniel Markovits, Michael Sandel, and David Brooks have argued that the mass alienation of the American general public from state institutions stems from the monopolization of political life by elites who attended Ivy League and other highly prestigious universities. Such institutions of higher learning admit a tiny fraction of the applicant pool, which is already highly skewed toward the wealthiest families in America. The result is the reinforcement of an insular ruling class possessing a limited range of real-life experience, trained to accept establishment liberal politics, and confident that they are indeed "the best and the brightest" members of society. It's no wonder that so many ordinary people see Harvard, Yale, and Stanford graduates as stuck up and out of touch – yet they go on to dominate our leading financial firms, our editorial boards, our federal judiciary, and our Supreme Court.[6]

As in the case of radical democratic critiques of the administrative state, criticism of meritocracy has long historical antecedents. And as with proposals to institutionalize radical democracy, the solutions to the problem offered by these critics also fail the test of political feasibility. An end to "legacy" admissions favoring the children of alumni of elite universities certainly makes good sense, as does a shift in public support away from such bastions of privilege to the public universities and vocational schools that currently educate the vast majority of America's college population. Yet none of this will prevent wealthy families from socializing their children to see elite university attendance as a prerequisite to social success – or from spending copious amounts of money on preparing them to "excel" in ways that are attractive to Ivy League admissions committees. The recent Supreme Court decision banning affirmative action in higher education will likely reinforce, not undermine, the perpetuation of elite privilege in the admissions process. Nor is there any realistic prospect that Harvard, Yale, and Stanford will begin to select their undergraduate class in part by lottery, as Sandel has proposed.

Beyond the impracticality of the critique of meritocracy lies a deeper problem: such criticism only reinforces the general contemporary bias against academic expertise and training that is at the root of the assault on the modern state. It's easy to criticize smug Harvard alumni who were born into privilege yet somehow still think that they are the most hardworking, "meritorious" members of society. But the overwhelming percentage of federal employees, judges, lawyers, public health officials, and other experts who run the modern state got their degrees at far less famous – yet equally excellent – places. The American university system has long been admired around the world not just because of the prominent achievements of faculty at Harvard and Yale, but also because students can study with top experts in every field at universities and colleges in every part of the country. Ironically, the critique of meritocratic rule formulated by Harvard professors like Markovits and Sandel will almost surely leave Harvard's own immense wealth and global status entirely unaffected – but it may well do a great deal of damage to faculty autonomy and academic freedom at the thousands of less famous public universities that actually educate most of our nation's civil servants.

In a world threatened by the global diffusion of patrimonial politics and the concomitant subordination and
dismantling of legal state agencies, progressive and
communitarian critiques of the administrative state simply
don't help. To cure the problem of mass disaffection with
government agencies, fostered by rightwing movements
with frankly antiliberal goals, they propose the further
disruption of both the modern state and the system
of higher education that provides much of its professional expertise. Instead, we propose precisely the opposite
approach, which is also logically much more straight-
forward: a true defense of the modern state must begin
with unabashed support for the state's role and importance
in a good society.

* * *

The time has clearly come for all of us who care about
the public good to renew our appreciation for what a
marvelous human invention the modern state truly is. As
scholars have shown, its appearance on the world stage
was nowhere guaranteed and required a combination
of institutional adaptation, compromise, bloodshed, and
almost always a measure of luck. Once ruined, will the
rule-of-law state ever reappear? Just because we may need
and want the modern state does not mean we will get it.
Failure is an option.[7]
We are used to extoling the discoveries of famous entrepreneurs and scientists, with schoolchildren learning at an
early age about Thomas Edison's patents or the discovery of
the double-helix structure of DNA by Francis Crick, James
Watson, and Rosalind Franklin. We are less accustomed
to celebrating political inventions like the modern army,
the modern political party, and the modern state itself. We
tend to think of large-scale political phenomena like these
as "structures" that have somehow emerged spontaneously

– and perhaps malevolently – from hidden forces we don't understand. Such thinking contributes in its own way to the propagation of conspiracy theories like the concept of the deep state. Yet all these political organizations are just as assuredly the product of human innovation as the technological and scientific breakthroughs we routinely attribute to individual creativity. The modern state was created in the Middle Ages, and later spread through Europe and beyond, not because of some supernatural historical force, but rather because both rulers and ordinary people discovered that it helped to solve problems of coordination and communication that had hindered large-scale human cooperation since prehistoric times.

This sense of historical perspective is badly missing from our current debates about the future of the global political order. We endlessly debate whether to have "more state" or "more market" determining the allocation of resources, not recognizing that neither "the state" nor "the market" was capable of allocating social goods in a reliable way before the modern era. The very quest to find a proper "balance" between the state and the market, in this sense, is a luxury of modern times – and one we can easily squander. When the state as we know it disintegrates and is replaced by the arbitrary rule of powerful men and their political "households," it will become perfectly clear that neither "libertarianism" nor "social democracy" is attainable – only the politics of survival for oneself and one's loved ones in a violent world of competing clans and empires.

It is in this context that a renewed call for a new generation to embrace public service becomes especially urgent. Critics of our current meritocratic state order seem not to notice that it is rapidly dying anyway, for simple demographic reasons. In state agencies at the federal, state, and local level alike, severe workforce

150

problems are becoming endemic. Those who remain on the job are more stressed out than ever, inspiring many to consider early retirement – creating a vicious cycle. Obviously, continuous political attacks on state workers as unaccountable supporters of the "deep state" don't help remedy this situation. As one Minnesota state worker described the difficulty in finding new recruits: "It's terrifying, if I'm being honest ... People just don't know about the opportunities that exist. It's a great work force, it's a great field to be in, but it's a really intimidating thing that isn't portrayed accurately in the movies and the media."[8]

One implication of this observation is the need to reverse the erosion of status attributed to public employment compared to that of the private sector. Such a reversal of esteem is possible. Japan and Germany, for example, have long had thriving market economies with a public sector that regularly draws the society's most talented and ambitious employees. Senior civil servants in Japan have, in fact, historically moved from long state careers into private industry. Not every country needs to replicate this model, but it does show that a high-status public sector is perfectly compatible with capitalism.

Recruitment of the next generation of public servants is vital for yet another reason: American society, like societies around the world, is rapidly becoming more diverse. Demographers estimate that the United States will become a majority–minority nation sometime in the 2040s, and this is already a reality in important states like California, Texas, and (as of 2021) Maryland. Remarkably, the federal workforce today is nearly as diverse as the population it serves – but few young people are aware of this fact. And there are still significant racial and gender disparities in the leadership of federal agencies and the judiciary. The clear lesson to be drawn is that the US needs to mount a concerted public relations campaign that attracts young people from diverse backgrounds to apply to colleges and universities, to gain expertise in fields of particular importance to the public sector, and then to apply to fill the growing vacancies in state employment. It is hard, in this cynical age, to imagine a new US president stirring the hearts of the youth with proclamations like the famous line in John F. Kennedy's inaugural speech: "Ask not what your country can do for you – ask what you can do for your country." But such a ringing, unmodified embrace of the value of public service has never been more warranted.[9]

* * *

Lastly, we return to the global dimension of the assault on the modern state. We have argued in this book that the original template for antimodern state-building in the twenty-first century emerged in Putin's Russia. Certainly, long before Putin's emergence, there were many "populist" critics of the liberal establishment in democracies throughout the West. Yet before Putin succeeded in building an internationally powerful patrimonial regime in the 2000s, antiliberal politicians lacked a model for seizing and consolidating political power in a way that might truly displace the post-World War II political order. As Putin's Russia grew rich on energy exports, crushed its internal opponents, and began to exert its geopolitical influence in Eurasia and then further afield, enemies of the modern "administrative state" began to take notice. Supporters of strong executive power admired Putin's "macho" image, comparing him favorably to legally constrained, cautious liberal executives like Barack Obama. Christian nationalists noted Putin's close alliance with the Russian Orthodox Church as well as his antipathy toward "sinful" lifestyles, and they wondered if a similar fusion of Christianity and state power might be forged in the liberal West. Even libertarians found reasons to like Putin's regime, which appeared to share their disdain for "bureaucrats" who wished to dictate the minute details of one's personal life. Of course, Putin's regime also spent billions of rubles actively promoting pro-Russian propaganda among all these groups. But Russian influence campaigns worked so well only because the cultural affinities between them and Russia's patrimonial regime were already so strong.

The links between the Kremlin and would-be patrimonial political groupings in countries around the world remain robust today. In May 2023, a Russian "sanctions list" of 500 Americans, barring them from travel to Russia, included some odd names: Brad Raffensperger, Letitia James, and Michael Byrd. Raffensperger, Georgia's secretary of state, refused in a recorded telephone call with Donald Trump to "find" another 11,780 votes in his favor. James was New York State's attorney general who initiated criminal proceedings against Trump for civil fraud. Byrd was the officer who shot and killed Ashli Babbitt as she participated in the invasion of the US Capitol on January 6, 2021. None of these people had anything to do with Russia policy. Apparently, Putin came to see Trump's enemies as his own. And a deep divide emerged within the Republican Party between what remained of the hawkish anti-Russian establishment and those who joined Trump in embracing Putin's picture of the war in Ukraine.

The full-scale Russian invasion of Ukraine must therefore be understood not only as a vital struggle for the future of democracy. It also marks a potential turning point in the global battle between patrimonialism and the modern state. As we have seen, Putin tried to install a crony state in Kyiv for decades – without success. The Ukrainian people's collective, heroic resistance to becoming another satrapy of the twenty-first century Russian Empire gave the West a chance to block the future geopolitical diffusion of the patrimonial regime type. If Ukraine succeeds in establishing a sovereign rule-of-law state, Putin's project to undermine the global liberal order will be fatally undermined. If Russia instead crushes Ukraine's independence and installs a Kremlin loyalist in power, the balance of power in the rest of Europe may well tip toward patrimonialism as the dominant principle of state legitimacy. Some patrimonial regimes, like the budding one in Poland until its electoral defeat in October 2023, may still see Russia as an enemy – but the resulting geopolitical struggle will no longer be one aiming to unify rule-of-law, constitutional states against the threat of Putinism. Instead, the world will witness a chaotic free-for-all among competing visions of national patrimony – precisely the situation that generated World War I at the beginning of the twentieth century.

The foreign policy priority to resist the global patrimonial wave has taken on even greater urgency due to recent developments in the People's Republic of China under Xi Jinping. Since the days of Mao Zedong, China has benefited from a well-developed centralized state that is capable of carrying out chosen government policies across its vast territory. The Chinese party-state is, of course, also ruthless in its repression of opposition groups and relentless in its attacks on individual human rights. Yet China's rise to global power nevertheless owes a great deal to the comparative reliability of its state apparatus to pursue collective goals. Advocates of neoliberal market fundamentalism have been surprised for decades about the relative effectiveness of the Chinese model of state-guided marketization.

Having said that, Xi's vision for China's future has increasingly shifted in a patrimonial direction. Instead of abiding by legal norms governing the length of terms in executive office for Chinese leaders, Xi chose in 2022 to stay on as general secretary of the Chinese Communist Party past the established limit of two five-year terms.

Increasingly, Xi poses in Chinese propaganda as the "father of the nation," who alone can ensure China's future unity, security, and prosperity. He insists on absolute personal loyalty, quickly purging high-ranking communist party officials who run afoul of the Xi party line. And he mandates that his governing philosophy, so-called Xi Jinping Thought, be memorized not only by party members but also by ordinary citizens across China. Chinese citizens are even encouraged to download a special smartphone app that offers ideological training and weekly quizzes, with points awarded for correct answers to questions about Xi's life and political pronouncements. All of these developments threaten to lead China toward the type of "communist familialism" practiced in Nicolae Ceausescu's Romania during the Cold War or in North Korea under the Kim dynasty today.[10]

As the Chinese state begins to shift from one primarily built on Leninist party bureaucracy to one centered on Xi's personal authority, it also has begun to suffer from the typical pathologies of patrimonial states. Like Putin, Johnson, and Trump, Xi's response to the coronavirus pandemic was abysmal, veering from early denial about the spread of COVID-19 from its origins in Wuhan, to a "zero Covid" policy involving overly strict lockdown rules that trapped hundreds of millions of Chinese citizens in their apartments for months at a time, and then to a sudden reopening that allowed the virus to spread through the population like wildfire. Xi's unexplained purges of top officials, including his own handpicked foreign minister, defense minister, and the head of China's Rocket Forces, threatened to undermine morale and cohesion in the nation's security services. Xi's patrimonial turn also helps to explain his otherwise seemingly odd "friendship" with Vladimir Putin, with whom he pledged a strategic partnership with "no limits." Xi, like Putin, wants to see the US-led global liberal order overturned in favor of a world of states organized around the principle of personal loyalty, and this goes a long way toward explaining his unwillingness to criticize Russian conduct during its war against Ukraine.

Seeing the defense of rule-of-law states, and not only democracy, as a central plank of US foreign policy would be salutary for an additional reason: this would help to correct the common American mistake of assuming that "democracy" will break out as soon as an old dictatorship is defeated. Critics of the US invasions of Afghanistan and Iraq tend to conclude that we should avoid any future efforts at "nation-building." The real problem in American strategy is that there has been far too little understanding of the necessity of post-conflict state-building. In the case of post-Saddam Iraq, the US presided over the disintegration of the state bureaucracy and military in a misguided effort to purge former Ba'athists. The result was a catastrophic loss of central control that undermined public safety and damaged the economy, creating a fertile recruiting environment for shadowy militias and Islamist extremists. Even in the case of Afghanistan, where, for historical and cultural reasons, the task of building up a coherent state bureaucracy will always be daunting, far too little attention was paid after 2001 to recruiting and training new Afghan state officials with enough of a professional ethos to resist the worst forms of corruption. As in Russia during the 1990s, prolonged political and economic uncertainty in postwar Afghanistan and Iraq only increased social support for alternative forms of traditional order that might put an end to the chaos – with catastrophic effects on America's global reputation and future credibility.

* * *

We hope that we have made a persuasive case for renewed attention to the assault on the modern state as a central trend of the early twenty-first century. We've emphasized that this threat is different from the equally worrisome trend of global democratic decline. But what about the future of democracy, then? How might defending the modern state from its enemies contribute to preserving the integrity of democratic elections and citizenship?

We share the concerns of our political science colleagues about democracy's uncertain future. It's hard not to be pessimistic. We may not live in an age of strutting fascists or menacing colonels in sunglasses, but we do inhabit a world in which popularly elected politicians increasingly try to stay in power by chipping away at the institutional constraints that undergird democratic rule. As Levitsky and Ziblatt put it *How Democracies Die*: "Some of these leaders dismantle democracy quickly, as Hitler did in the wake of the 1933 Reichstag fire in Germany. More often, though, democracies erode slowly, in barely visible steps." These new authoritarians do not tear up constitutions, but they do subvert them from within. They attack judges, election officials, professional journalists, and even the postal service, hollowing out the institutions that democracy needs to function.

Worse yet, in the years since Levitsky and Ziblatt wrote their seminal book in 2018, violence has reentered the political scene. Donald Trump's incitement of his mob to attack the US Capitol on January 6, 2021, and his multiple threats in the years thereafter, have provided a disturbing model. Trailing his opponent in his failed reelection bid, Brazil's far-right president Jair Bolsonaro attacked the judges on his country's electoral court. "Our generation can't be remembered in the future as one that had a chance to do something but cowered before two or three people," Bolsonaro declared. "Buy your weapons, that's in the Bible." It was unfortunately no surprise when, after their hero's defeat in the Brazilian presidential elections of October 2022, Bolsonaro's supporters stormed the Brazilian capital in direct emulation of the January 6 insurrection.[11]

But thankfully, political violence within long-established democracies has so far been the exception. And there is a difference, some have noted, between how extremist parties campaign versus how they rule. Extremist campaign rhetoric may indeed be scary, but such parties frequently become more moderate once they are in office: their bark is bigger than their bite. In a survey of West European antiliberal parties ranging from France's National Front to the Sweden Democrats, Sheri Berman finds that "whether extremist parties become significant threats to democracy depends less on the parties and more on the nature of the democracies they face." Where democratic institutions and values are strong, extremists moderate their positions and behavior because they want to win elections. The clear conclusion is that antidemocratic politicians and movements can only be countered successfully when a country's legal, procedural framework remains intact – and this, in turn, depends upon the continuing profession-alism of countless state officials and judges who enforce democratic rules at the federal, state, and local levels, even when they come under immense personal pressure. Modern representative democracy, in short, requires the modern state.[12]

We have been careful to distinguish between the assault on the modern state and democratic erosion because they are different things and require different remedies. Even so, these two pathologies tend to reinforce each other. The contemporary assault on the administrative state is bad for democracy for the same reasons it is bad for the environment, the safety of our food and water, the economy, and public health. Elections and civil rights are public goods that are not somehow spontaneously provided. It follows then that the state's decay and democracy's decay will go hand in hand. Defending democracy means defending the state.

The converse is also true: if we want to preserve the modern state, maintaining the constitutional framework for popular voting and participation is vitally important. While history does provide some examples of authoritarian regimes that rule through effective, uncorrupted bureaucracies, this is the exception and not the rule. And the new authoritarians threatening democracy today are hardly paragons of civic virtue. If they emerge triumphant, they will surely continue to promote their sycophants and cronies to key state positions, while dismantling what is left of the civil service and independent judiciary. While the erosion of the modern state can take place under democratic as well as authoritarian leaders, that hardly means that democratic elections no longer matter. The fact that, notwithstanding all their protests and maneuvering, both Trump and Bolsonaro were genuinely defeated by their opponents at the ballot box has played a pivotal role in preventing the consolidation of patrimonial rule in the United States and Brazil thus far.

All of this suggests that there should be a strong alliance between supporters of democracy and those of us who value the contributions of the modern state to our safety, security, and prosperity. And we will certainly need unity in the struggles ahead. What is often called the "global liberal order" is essentially the product of long-term international cooperation among modern states sharing a basic commitment to the domestic rule of law. If too many of its constituent powers abandon that commitment and embrace the patrimonial politics of premodern times, the global order will surely crumble. The world that would then emerge would be incomparably more violent, insecure, and undemocratic, eliminating all hope of organizing global cooperation to keep our planet from a climate catastrophe. Preserving the modern state at this critical juncture may thus determine the fate of humanity itself.

Notes

Chapter 1: At the Precipice

1 Oliver Wainwright, "Seasteading – a Vanity Project for the Rich or the Future of Humanity?" *Guardian*, June 24, 2020; Max Matza, "What is the Sovereign Citizen Movement?" *BBC News*, August 5, 2020.

2 Salena Zito, "DeSantis: People Don't Want 'Agenda being Shoved Down their Throat'," *New York Post*, February 18, 2023; Doug Thompson, "Design Error Blamed for Essay Requirement on What Accomplishment of Arkansas Governor that Applicants 'Admire the Most,'" *Arkansas Democrat Gazette*, April 14, 2023.

3 Frank Morris, "USDA Research Agencies 'Decimated' by Forced Move. Undoing the Damage Won't be Easy," *National Public Radio*, February 2, 2021.

4 Julia Adams, *The Familial State: Ruling Families and Merchant Capitalism in Early Modern Europe*, Cornell University Press, 2005. The metaphor of "thumbs" and "fingers" is taken from Charles Lindblom, *Politics and Markets: The World's Political-Economic Systems*, Basic Books, 1977.

5 Thomas Hobbes, *Leviathan*, Pearson Longman, 2008 [1651].

6 For the argument that powerful new regime types typically emerge from unexpected and marginalized places, see Ken Jowitt, *New World Order: The Leninist Extinction*, University of California Press, 1992.

Chapter 2: The Deep State Bogeyman

1 Sheelah Kolhatkar, "A Tycoon's Deep-State Conspiracy Dive," *New Yorker*, December 7, 2020.
2 Jane Kramer, "The Money Behind the Big Lie," *New Yorker*, August 2, 2021; Doug Bock Clark, Alexandra Berzon, and Kirsten Berg, "Building the 'Big Lie': Inside the Creation of Trump's Stolen Election Myth," *ProPublica*, April 26, 2022; Barbara Sprunt, "Inside the 'Unhinged' West Wing Meeting on Dec. 18," NPR, July 12, 2022.
3 Jerome R. Corsi, *Killing the Deep State: The War to Save President Trump*, Humanix Books, 2018; Jason Chaffetz, *The Deep State: How an Army of Bureaucrats Protected Barack Obama and Is Working to Destroy the Trump Agenda*, Broadside Books, 2018; Lt. Col. Robert Maginnis, *The Deeper State: Inside the War on Trump by Corrupt Elites, Secret Societies in the Builders of an Imminent Final Empire*, Defender Publishing, 2017. For an excellent overview of the main themes of this literature, see Robert B. Horwitz, "Trump and the 'Deep State'," *Policy Studies*, 42/5–6 (2021), pp. 473–490.
4 Mallory Newell, "More than 1 in 3 Americans Believe a 'Deep State' is Working to Undermine Trump," *Ipsos*, December 30, 2020; Rebecca Morin, "Poll: Majority Believe 'Deep State' Manipulates US Policies," *Politico*, March 19, 2018.
5 Pew Research Center, "Trust in Government 1958–2022," June 6, 2022; Pew Research Center, "The State of Personal Trust," July 22, 2019.
6 James H. Meyer, "Politics as Usual: Ciller, Refah and Susurluk: Turkey's Troubled Democracy," *East European Quarterly*, 32 (1999), pp. 489–502; Methap Soyler, *The Turkish Deep State: State Consolidation, Civil–Military Relations and Democracy*, Routledge, 2015.
7 Daniel Dombey, "Turkey Begins Trial of General over 'Postmodern' Coup," *Financial Times*, September 2, 2013; Dexter Filkins, "Turkey's Thirty-Year Old Coup," *New Yorker*, October 10, 2016.

8 David M. Faris, "Deep State, Deep Crisis: Egypt and American Foreign Policy," *Middle East Studies*, 20/4 (2013), pp. 99–110; Sanim Vakil and Hossein Rasam, "Iran's Next Supreme Leader: The Islamic Republic after Khamenei," *Foreign Affairs*, 96/3 (May/June 2017), pp. 76–86; Jean-Pierre Filiu, *From Deep State to Islamic State: The Arab Counter-Revolution and its Jihadi Legacy*, Oxford University Press, 2015.

9 Mike Lofgren, *The Deep State: The Fall of the Constitution and the Rise of a Shadow Government*, Viking, 2016; Peter Dale Scott, *The American Deep State: Big Money, Big Oil and the Struggle for American Democracy*, Rowman & Littlefield, 2015.

10 Virgil, "The Deep State v. Donald Trump," *Breitbart News*, December 12, 2016.

11 Mark Hensch, "Gingrich: 'The Deep State Exists'," *The Hill*, March 14, 2017; Peter Baker, Lara Jakes, Sharon LaFraniere, and Edward Wong, "Trump's War on the 'Deep State' Turns against him," *New York Times*, October 23, 2019.

12 Matthew Nussbaum, "Park Service Behaved Appropriately Regarding Trump Crowd Reports, Watchdog Finds," *Politico*, June 26, 2017.

13 Martin Pengelly, "Fox Host Blames 'Deep State' for Bannon Arrest – Bannon Says that's for 'Nut Cases'," *Guardian*, August 21, 2020; Philip Rucker and Robert Costa, "Bannon Vows a Daily Fight for 'Deconstruction of the Administrative State," *Washington Post*, February 23, 2017.

14 Andrew Marantz, "Does Hungary Offer a Glimpse of our Authoritarian Future?" *New Yorker*, June 27, 2022; Adam Forrest, "Brexit: Boris Johnson Suggests Keir Starmer and 'Deep State' Plotting to Take UK Back into EU," *Independent*, July 18, 2022; Stefania Maurizi, "Edward Snowden: Poisoning People Who Are Long Out of Their Service Is Contemptible," *La Repubblica*, March 19, 2018.

15 Ayn Rand, *Atlas Shrugged*, Random House, 1957; Friedrich Hayek, *The Road to Serfdom*, University of Chicago Press, 1944.

16 Jeff Walker, *The Ayn Rand Cult*, Open Court, 1999; Jennifer

Burns, *The Goodness of the Market: Ayn Rand and the American Right*, Oxford University Press, 2009.

17 Bruce Caldwell, *Hayek's Challenge: An Intellectual Biography of F.A. Hayek*, University of Chicago Press, 2004; FRED, "Federal Net Outlays as a Percent of Gross Domestic Product," St. Louis Fed, March 30, 2023.

18 Jane Meyer, *Dark Money: The Hidden History of the Billionaires Behind the Radical Right*, Doubleday, 2016; Brian Doherty, *Radicals for Capitalism: A Freewheeling History of the Modern American Libertarian Movement*, Public Affairs 2007; Charles Koch, *Good Profit: How Creating Value for Others Built One of the World's Most Successful Companies*, Crown Business, 2015.

19 Benjamin Wallace-Wells, "The Rise of the Thielists," *New Yorker*, May 13, 2021; Deepa Seetharaman and Emily Glazer, "How Mark Zuckerberg Learned Politics," *Wall Street Journal*, October 16, 2020; Jeremy W. Peters, "The Elusive Politics of Elon Musk," *New York Times*, April 16, 2022; David E. Broockman, Gregory Ferenstein, and Neil Malhotra, "Predispositions and the Behavior of American Economic Elites: Evidence from Technology Entrepreneurs," *American Journal of Political Science*, 63/1 (January 2019), pp. 212–233.

20 Sarah Posner, "How the Christian Right Helped Foment Insurrection," *Rolling Stone*, January 31, 2021.

21 Philip S. Gorski and Samuel L. Perry, *The Flag and the Cross: White Christian Nationalism and the Threat to American Democracy*, Oxford University Press, 2022.

22 Michael Luciano, "Orbán Gets Standing Ovation at CPAC after Declaring Marriage is 'The Union of One Man and One Woman'," *Mediaite*, August 4, 2022; Maite Fernández Simon, "'A Woman is a Woman, A Man is a Man': Putin Compares Gender Nonconformity to the Coronavirus Pandemic," *Washington Post*, December 23, 2021.

23 Jay Michaelson, "The Secrets of Leonard Leo, The Man Behind Trump's Supreme Court Pick," *Daily Beast*, July 24, 2018.

24 Jeffrey Crouch, Mark J. Rozell, and Mitchel A. Sollenberger,

The Unitary Executive Theory: A Danger to Constitutional Government, University of Kansas Press, 2020.

25 John A. Farrell, "Watergate Created Roger Stone. Trump Completed Him," *Politico Magazine*, January 29, 2019.

26 Mark J. Rozell and Mitchel A. Sollenberger, "The Unitary Executive Theory and the Bush Legacy," in Donald R. Kelley and Todd G. Sheilds, eds., *Taking the Measure: The Presidency of George W. Bush*, pp. 36–54.

27 Michael Brice-Saddler, "While Bemoaning Muller Probe, Trump Falsely Says the Constitution Gives Him 'The Right to Do Whatever I Want," *Washington Post*, July 23, 2019.

Chapter 3: Beyond the Democracy Debate

1 Sumit Ganguly, "India's 'Electoral Autocracy' Hits Back," *Foreign Policy*, March 19, 2021.

2 Laurenz Gehrke, "Hungary No Longer a Democracy: Report," *Politico*, May 6, 2020.

3 David Collier and Steven Levitsky, "Democracy with Adjectives: Conceptual Innovation in Comparative Research," *World Politics*, 49/3 (1997), pp. 430–451.

4 Andrew Janos, *Politics and Paradigms*, Stanford University Press, 1986.

5 Steven Levitsky and Daniel Ziblatt, *How Democracies Die*, Penguin Random House, 2018.

6 Weber's writings on this are mostly concentrated in his two volume *Economy and Society: Outline of Interpretive Sociology*, edited and translated by Guenther Roth and Claus Wittich, University of California, Press, 1978. An indispensable overview remains Reinhard Bendix, *Max Weber: An Intellectual Portrait*, University of California Press, 1978.

7 Mounira M. Charrad and Julia Adams, "Introduction: Patrimonialism, Past and Present," *Annals of the American Academy of Political and Social Science*, 636/1 (2011), pp. 6–15.

8 Richard Pipes, *Russia under the Old Regime*, Simon & Schuster, 1974.

9 Boris Mironov, *Rossiiskaia Imperiia: Ot Traditsii k Modernu*, vol. 2, Dmitrii Bulanin, 2015.

10 Julia Adams, *The Familial State: Ruling Families and Merchant Capitalism in Early Modern Europe*, Cornell University Press, 2005.

11 Ryszard Kapuściński, *The Emperor: Downfall of an Autocrat*, Harcourt, Brace, Jovanovich, 1978, pp. 30–31.

12 Jonathan Hartlyn, "The Trujillo Regime in the Dominican Republic," in H.E. Chehabi and Juan Linz, eds., *Sultanistic Regimes*, Johns Hopkins University Press, 1998.

13 Mark R. Thompson, "The Marcos Regime in the Philippines," in Chehabi and Linz, eds., *Sultanistic Regimes*.

14 Mancur Olson, *The Logic of Collective Action*, Harvard University Press, 1971.

15 Wolfgang J. Mommsen, "Max Weber and the Regeneration of Russia," *Journal of Modern History*, 69/1 (1997), pp. 1–17.

Chapter 4: How Vladimir Putin Resurrected Tsarism

1 Robert S. Mueller III, *The Mueller Report*, Scribner, 2019.

2 Stephen Kotkin, *Magnetic Mountain: Stalinism as a Civilization*, University of California Press, 1997.

3 George Breslauer, "In Defense of Sovietology," *Post-Soviet Affairs*, 8/3 (1992), pp. 197–238; Alexei Yurchak, *Everything Was Forever, Until It Was No More: The Last Soviet Generation*, Princeton University Press, 2005.

4 Stephen E. Hanson, "Gorbachev: The Last True Leninist Believer?" in Daniel Chirot, ed., *The Crisis of Leninism and the Decline of the Left*, University of Washington Press, 1991, pp. 33–59.

5 For Putin's reaction to the fall of the Berlin Wall, see Natalia Gevorkian, Natalia Timakova, and A.V. Kolesnikov, eds., *First Person: An Astonishingly Frank Self-Portrait by Russia's President*, Public Affairs, 2000.

6 Stephen Crowley, *Hot Coal, Cold Steel: Russian and Ukrainian Workers from the End of the Soviet Union to the*

Post-Communist Transformations, University of Michigan Press, 1997.

7 Debra Javeline, *Protest and the Politics of Blame: The Russian Response to Unpaid Wages*, University of Michigan Press, 2003; Raimondo Lanza, "A State of Mind: How Conspiracy Theories Became the Kremlin's Ideology," *Aspenia Online*, April 4, 2023.

8 Giovanni Capoccia and R. Daniel Kelemen, "The Study of Critical Junctures: Theory, Narrative, and Counterfactuals in Historical Institutionalism," *World Politics*, 59/3 (2007), pp. 341–369; Serge Schmemann, "Yeltsin is Telling Russians to Brace for Sharp Reform," *New York Times*, October 29, 1991.

9 Francis Fukuyama, "The End of History?" *National Interest*, 16/4 (1989), pp. 3–18; Robert J. Samuelson, "The Peace Dividend: If the Budget Balances, Gorbachev Deserves More Credit than Clinton or Gingrich," *Newsweek*, 131/4 (1998), p. 49.

10 Kathryn Hendley, "'Telephone Law' and the 'Rule of Law': The Russian Case," *Hague Journal on the Rule of Law*, 1/2 (2009), pp. 241–262; Juliet Johnson, *A Fistful of Rubles: The Rise and Fall of the Russian Banking System*, Cornell University Press, 2000; Stephen Wegren, *Land Reform in Russia: Institutional Design and Behavioral Responses*, Yale University Press, 2009; Yoshiko Herrera, *Mirrors of the Economy: National Accounts and International Norms in Russia and Beyond*, Cornell University Press, 2017.

11 Jeffrey Sachs, *Poland's Jump to the Market Economy*, MIT Press, 1994.

12 Steven L. Solnick, *Stealing the State: Control and Collapse in Soviet Institutions*, Harvard University Press, 1998.

13 Chrystia Freeland, *Sale of the Century: Russia's Wild Ride from Communism to Capitalism*, Crown Business, 2000; David Woodruff, *Money Unmade: Barter and the Fate of Russian Capitalism*, Cornell University Press, 1999.

14 Philip Hanson et al., *Russia and the WTO: A Progress Report*, NBR Special Report No. 12, National Bureau of Asian Research, March 1, 2007.

15 Jeffrey Tayler, "Russia is Finished," *The Atlantic*, May 2001.

16 Jonathan Steele, "Yeltsin Sacks Russian PM to Install Ex-Spy as his Heir," *Guardian*, August 9, 1999; Peter Baker and Susan Glasser, *Kremlin Rising: Vladimir Putin's Russia and the End of Revolution*, Scribner, 2005.

17 John Dunlop, *The Moscow Bombings of September 1999: Examinations of Russian Terrorist Attacks at the Onset of Vladimir Putin's Rule*, Ibidem-Verlag, 2014.

18 Gevorkian, Timakova, and Kolesnikov, *First Person*; Steven Lee Myers, *The New Tsar: The Rise and Reign of Vladimir Putin*, Simon & Schuster, 2015, p. 159.

19 Oil prices taken from "Europe Brent Spot Price FOB," US Energy Information Administration.

20 Richard Rose and Neil Munro, *Elections Without Order: Russia's Challenge to Vladimir Putin*, Cambridge University Press, 2002.

21 Brian D. Taylor, *The Code of Putinism*, Oxford University Press, 2018; Karen Dawisha, *Putin's Kleptocracy: Who Owns Russia?* Simon & Schuster, 2014; Catherine Belton, *Putin's People: How the KGB Took Back Russia and Then Took on the West*, Farrar, Straus & Giroux, 2020; Fiona Hill and Clifford Gaddy, *Mr. Putin: Operative in the Kremlin*, Brookings, 2013.

22 Pauline Jones Luong and Erika Weinthal, *Oil Is Not a Curse: Ownership Structure and Institutions in Soviet Successor States*, Cambridge University Press, 2010.

23 "Toxic Tea: Multiple Russians Hit by Suspected Poisonings," Associated Press, August 20, 2020.

24 Michael McFaul, "Russia's Road to Autocracy," *Journal of Democracy*, 32/4 (October 2021), pp. 11–26; Miriam Elder, "Vladimir Putin Accuses Hillary Clinton of Encouraging Protests," *Guardian*, December 8, 2011.

25 Valerie Sperling, *Sex, Politics, and Putin: Political Legitimacy in Russia*, Oxford University Press, 2014; Gleb Bryanski, "Russian Patriarch Calls Putin Era 'Miracle of God'," *Reuters World News*, February 8, 2012; Joshua Yaffa, "Vladimir Putin Positions Himself to Become Russia's Eternal Leader," *New Yorker*, March 11, 2020.

Chapter 5: The Wave: From East to West

1 Tobias Jones, "How Matteo Salvini Became Putin's Man in Europe," *Prospect*, August 30, 2019; Adam Ganucheau, "How Donald Trump and Nigel Farage Met in Mississippi," *Mississippi Today*, November 15, 2016.
2 Megan Stack, "Chechen Tiger without a Chain," *Los Angeles Times*, June 17, 2008; Joshua Yaffa, "Putin's Dragoon: Is the Ruler of Chechnya Out of Control?" *New Yorker*, June 31, 2016.
3 Valerie Hopkins, "Kazakhstan's Longtime Leader Is Gone, but Still Seemingly Everywhere," *New York Times*, January 25, 2022; Zoya Sheftalovich, "Belarus's Lukashenko: 'The Only Mistake We Made' Was Not Finishing Off Ukraine in 2014," *Politico.eu*, June 2, 2023.
4 Mario Puzo, *The Godfather*, Putnam, 1969.
5 Olga Onuch and Henry E. Hale, *The Zelensky Effect*, Oxford University Press, 2023.
6 Lucan Way, *Pluralism by Default: Weak Autocrats and the Rise of Competitive Politics*, Johns Hopkins University Press, 2016; Henry Hale, *Patronal Politics: Eurasian Regime Dynamics in Comparative Perspective*, Cambridge University Press, 2015.
7 Paul Manafort, *Political Prisoner: Persecuted, Prosecuted, but Not Silenced*, Skyhorse Publishing, 2022, p. 215.
8 Serhii Plokhy, *The Russo-Ukrainian War: The Return of History*, W.W. Norton & Company.
9 Gwendolyn Sasse, *Der Krieg Gegen die Ukraine: Hintergründe, Ereignisse, Folgen*, C.H. Beck, 2022.
10 Milada Vachudova, *Europe Undivided: Democracy, Leverage, and Integration after Communism*, Oxford University Press, 2005; Wade Jacoby, "Tutors and Pupils: International Organizations, Central European Elites, and Western Models," *Governance*, 14/2 (2002), pp. 169–200.
11 Charlie Campbell, "Viktor Orban Is Set for a Fourth Term as Hungary's Prime Minister: That Could Be a Boost for Putin," *Time*, April 3, 2022; Ákos Keller-Alánt, Tibor Rácz, and Krisztián Simon, "How the Hungarian 'Zuckerberg' Is

Keeping Orbán's System Alive," *Heinrich Böll Stiftung*, May 3, 2017.

12 "Orbán Viktor családjának látható vagyona hamarosan átlépheti a 100 milliárdot," *hvg.hu*, June 2, 2023.

13 Dominic Spadacene, "Orbán Has Begun Taking Steps to Preserve His Power," *Euractiv*, September 27, 2022; Szijártó Hajnalka, "EU Withdraws Erasmus Support from Hungarian Foundation Universities," *Daily News Hungary*, September 1, 2023.

14 Nataliya Bugayova, "The Kremlin Targets Ukraine Through Hungary," *Institute for the Study of War*, October 31, 2017.

15 Andrew Marantz, "Does Hungary Offer a Glimpse of our Authoritarian Future?" *New Yorker*, June 27, 2022; Natalie Allison and Lamar Johnson, "Orbán Gets Warm CPAC Reception after 'Mixed Race' Speech Blowback," *Politico*, August 4, 2022.

16 Monika Sieradzka, *Deutsche Welle*, "'Kaczynski Tapes' Reveal Murky Business Dealings," January 31, 2019; "Kaczynski Accuses Brussels of Building 'Superstate'," *The First News*, October 20, 2021; Elisabeth Zerofsky, "Poland's War on Two Fronts," *New York Times*, April 4, 2023.

17 Nir Kedar, *David Ben-Gurion and the Foundation of Israeli Democracy*, Indiana University Press, 2021.

18 Maya Mark, "The Road Not Taken: Menachem Begin's Position on the Formation of a Democratic Regime for Israel," *Israel Studies Review*, 36/2 (2021); "From the Rule of Law to the Law of the Ruler: The Twofold Upheaval of the Israeli Right," *Israel Studies*, 28/3 (2023), pp. 4–18.

19 Gideon Rahat and Tamir Sheafer, "The Personalization of Politics: Israel, 1949–2003," *Political Communication*, 24/1 (2007), pp. 65–80.

20 Peggy Cidor, "Why the Right-Wing Mizrahi Vote Is Misunderstood in Israel," *Middle East Eye*, February 1, 2023; Sue Surkes, "Why the Left Keeps Failing in the Pro-Likud Periphery, Home to 25% of Israelis," *Times of Israel*, April 30, 2019.

21 Shalom Yerushalmi, "Source Close to Netanyahu Accuses US of Funding Rallies Against Judicial Overhaul," *Times*

of Israel, March 12, 2023; "Mass Protests Erupt After Netanyahu Fires Defense Chief" *CNBC*, March 26, 2023.

22 Anat Peled, "Resign or Resist Netanyahu's Judicial Coup from Within: The Dilemma Israeli Civil Servants Now Face," *Haaretz*, September 3, 2023.

23 Jon Stone, "Dominic Cummins Defends 'Eye-Test' Trip to Barnard Castle: 'I Would Have Made Up a Better Story'," *Independent*, May 26, 2021.

24 Mark Landler, "Boris Johnson Launches War on U.K.'s Own 'Deep State,'" *New York Times*, March 7, 2020; Andrew Kelsey, "Boris Johnson's New Lords Appointees Have Donated 17m to the Tory Party," *Open Democracy*, August 9, 2023.

25 John Bowden, "Watchdog Report: UK Government 'Badly Underestimated' Threat of Russian Interference," *The Hill*, July 7, 2021.

26 Ferdinand Mount, "Ruthless and Truthless," *London Review of Books*, 43/8 (2021).

27 Reality Check Team, "Northern Ireland Protocol: What Did Boris Johnson Say?" *BBC News*, June 2022; Patrick Wintour, "Viktor Orbán to Become Second EU Leader to Visit No 10 after Brexit," *Guardian*, May 27, 2021.

28 Leia Paxton, "'Stop Attacks!' Truss Braces for Westminster Revolt as Civil Service Tipped for Push Back," *Express*, September 5, 2022; Robert Shrimsley, "The Conservative War on Big Everything," *Financial Times*, July 26, 2023.

29 Brian Naylor, "An Acting Government for the Trump Administration," *NPR*, April 9, 2019.

30 Sean Reilly, "Dismissed EPA Science Advisers Gather in 'Unprecedented' Challenge to Trump Administration," *Science*, October 10, 2019.

31 David K. Li, "Birx on Trump's Disinfectant Proposal for Covid: 'I Didn't Know How to Handle that Episode'," *NBC News*, March 16, 2021.

32 Michael Shear, "Birx Testifies that Trump's White House Failed to Take Steps to Prevent More Virus Deaths," *New York Times*, October 26, 2021.

33 Anne Gearan, "'Surreal': Ivanka Trump Plays a Prominent Role in her Father's Historic Korea Trip," *Washington*

Post, June 30, 2019; Jonathan Swan, Kate Kelly, Maggie Haberman, and Mark Mazzetti, "Kushner Firm Got Hundreds of Millions from 2 Persian Gulf Nations," *New York Times*, March 30, 2023; Dylan Riley, "What is Trump?" *New Left Review*, November/December 2018.

34 Jonathan Swan, Charlie Savage, and Maggie Haberman, "Trump and Allies Forge Plans to Increase Presidential Power in 2025," *New York Times*, July 17, 2023.

35 Allan Smith, "Trump Zeroes in on a Key Target of his 'Retribution' Agenda: Government Workers," *NBC News*, April 26, 2023; Maura Zurick, "Trump Vows to 'Liberate' US from List of 'Villains' in Michigan Speech," *Newsweek*, June 26, 1993.

36 Zac Anderson, "Takeaways from Ron DeSantis' 'Confidential' Campaign Memo to Gain Ground on Donald Trump," *USA Today*, July 13, 2023.

Chapter 6: Reclaiming the Modern State

1 Michael Lewis, *The Fifth Risk: Undoing Democracy*, W.W. Norton & Company, 2018.

2 Brandon Gillespie, "DeSantis Torches Trump over COVID Lockdowns: 'He Turned the Country over to Fauci'," *Fox News*, May 25, 2023.

3 Ralph R. Smith, "2023 COLA and the Long-Expected Retirement Tsunami," *FedSmith.com*, March 17, 2022; Brandon Lardy, "The Federal Workforce Looks More Like the Country than You Might Think," *Partnership for Public Service*, May 10, 2023.

4 Tom Nichols, *The Death of Expertise: The Campaign Against Established Knowledge and Why it Matters*, Oxford University Press, 2017.

5 For a sympathetic review of the various proposals, see Bernardo Zacka, "Political Theory Rediscovers Public Administration," *Annual Review of Political Science*, 25 (2022), pp. 21–42; K. Sabeel Rahman, *Democracy Against Domination*, Oxford University Press, 2018, p. 15.

6 Michael J. Sandel, *The Tyranny of Merit: What's Become of the Common Good?* Picador, 2021; David Brooks, "What if We're the Bad Guys Here?" *New York Times*, August 2, 2023; Daniel Markovits, *The Meritocracy Trap: How America's Foundational Myth Feeds Inequality, Dismantles the Middle Class, and Devours the Elite*, Penguin Press, 2019.

7 Thomas Ertman, *Birth of the Leviathan: Building States and Regimes in Medieval and Early Modern Europe*, Cambridge University Press, 1997; Anna Grzymała-Busse, *Sacred Foundations: The Religious and Medieval Roots of the European State*, Princeton University Press, 2023.

8 Lydia DePillis, "Jobs Sit Empty in the Public Sector, So Unions Pitch in to Recruit," *New York Times*, July 27, 2023.

9 Lardy, "The Federal Workforce Looks More Like the Country than You Might Think."

10 Javier C. Hernández, "The Hottest App in China Teaches Citizens About Their Leader – And Yes, There's a Test," *New York Times*, April 7, 2019.

11 Simone Iglesias and Isadora Calumby, "Bolsonaro Is Stepping Up Radical Rhetoric in Brazil Election Run-Up," *Bloomberg*, August 10, 2022.

12 Sheri Berman, "How Western Europe's Far Right Moderated," *Persuasion*, July 26, 2023.

Index

Index

Index